THE GREAT TRAIN ROBBERY

A NEW HISTORY

JIM MORRIS

AMBERLEY

Front cover: Wider view of GVP coach (Mirrorpix); Evidential photograph of money from holdall (John Bailey Collection).

Back cover: Bucks Constabulary coat of arms (Claire Macdonald, courtesy of Michael Shaw).

First published 2013

Amberley Publishing
The Hill, Stroud
Gloucestershire, GL5 4EP

www.amberley-books.com

British Library Cataloguing in Publication Data.
A catalogue record for this book is available from the British Library.

ISBN 978 1 4456 0682 8
ISBN 978 1 4456 2056 5 (ebook)

Typeset in 10pt on 12pt Sabon.
Typesetting and Origination by Amberley Publishing.
Printed in the UK.

CONTENTS

INTRODUCTION

Overview

The Great Train Robbery – labelled 'great' by the media – was hailed as the crime of the century, and it was certainly a robbery on an unprecedented scale. It was planned, organised and carried out with a precision the military would have envied, and only a fraction of the money stolen has ever been accounted for. Most of those responsible (some were never caught) were given heavy prison sentences and some of the robbers and the police who pursued them have become household names. Books, films and documentaries have been produced in abundance, and it doesn't appear as though the 'legend' will ever fade.

Legend will always test the accuracy of memory and often a fact will grow away from its foundation, but it's usually in the recording of history that one finds a bias. One might even be encouraged to remember one thing and not something else, but hitherto 'neglected' facts will often speak with greater eloquence when they've been given the chance to mature. Fact and myth don't necessarily grow apart, rather they are pulled apart, and are nurtured separately; so most things in history are well worth a reappraisal.

With the coming of the Freedom of Information Act a lot of previously withheld documents and records became accessible to the public so one didn't need to rely so much on memories, word of mouth or on what newspapers said. The first three books about the Great Train Robbery were written by former police officers and a journalist – the wife of a barrister – so one is entitled to ask questions that may scrutinise the stance of their observations. But official documents may not be any better – far too many police investigations have been marred by fabricated evidence. So where does that leave the main event? History does rely on its recorder for accuracy, and accuracy relies on interpretation; so one cannot escape from the interpretation of police and writers. But it's the testing of what has been said over a prolonged period that may take us nearer the truth. It has been suggested that each new study tends to ask more questions than it answers, which only shows there are still questions to be asked.

I don't claim this book is intended to be the final word on the Great Train Robbery. I don't think that will ever be said.

The Venue

Buckinghamshire is north-west of London, and following the Second World War it consisted of both rural and urban areas; to the north the county was rural, but at its south-eastern border it joins Greater London/Middlesex, so is more commercialised and carries far more of the population. The county town is Aylesbury, which lies 40 miles from London. The county is around 720 square miles and by the 1960s, the population was close to 500,000; this was growing with the post-war London overspill which saw Buckinghamshire become popular, and the new town of Milton Keynes grow.

To look after the population there was the Buckinghamshire (Bucks) Constabulary, who had a modern headquarters in Aylesbury, and an establishment of 716 officers of which 536 were of the rank of sergeant and below. At night-time the total number of officers was only 55, of which the most senior was a sergeant, but the adequacy of this is borne out by the crime rate. However, on 8 August 1963 a crime was committed which all 55 officers would soon learn about, and their 660-odd colleagues, their civilian support workers and the entire population of Buckinghamshire, together with the rest of the country and a vast number of people worldwide. As soon as the press heard about the crime, it got a title: the Great Train Robbery.

But in rural Buckinghamshire that night the fifty-five officers (seven sergeants and forty-eight constables) were content to protect the public and, as far as I can gather, apart from the train raid little else happened. They covered five divisions: Aylesbury, Bletchley, Chesham, High Wycombe and what was known as the Slough division.

This was considered adequate, and if there was a major disaster there was what was known as a Mutual Aid Plan to put into operation. This meant the team could grow by another 135 officers up to the rank of chief inspector 'in short notice' and this could be again inflated by the availability of a further 260 officers within five hours. There were military personnel available too. The only problem with this plan was the interpretation of the term 'major disaster', and most folk saw it as an event which included a major loss of life; later, of course, it was to include a major crime!

Although crime was on the increase generally, in Buckinghamshire the figures for 1963 showed a 7 per cent increase from 1962 but the rate of detected crime remained the same at 52 per cent. (The Chief Constable of Leeds said in 1966 that in his city only a third of crimes were solved.) So under the chief constable, Brigadier John Cheney; the assistant chief constable, George Wilkinson; and the head of CID, Detective Superintendent Malcolm Fewtrell, crime in Buckinghamshire was no worse than in the rest of the country and better than in some areas.

The divisions mentioned above were further sub-divided and within the Aylesbury division was the Linslade sub-division, which was further broken down into six beats. The total establishment for this sub-division in 1963 was an inspector assisted by two sergeants and ten constables. A car with a radio was the main vehicle but there were also four motorcycles, which were not equipped with radios. In those days, communications between officers and stations were not nearly as sophisticated as they are today, and often once an officer was out on his beat then he was largely alone, though he had a whistle and there were police boxes, and he would meet his sergeant at a pre-arranged time and place. The sub-division covered roughly 68 square miles and about 13,000 souls were resident. There were over 200 farms and smallholdings and two disused RAF airfields – a fairly common feature of the landscape in those days.

Also common before the contemporary review of the railway network under Dr Beeching were railway lines. In the Linslade sub-division was the main London to Glasgow railway line, which fortunately managed to avoid Dr Beeching's cuts. This line passed through 12 miles of the sub-division and there was a station at Cheddington. The sub-division is broken down into beats and it was the Cheddington beat that saw the robbery. The beat hosted 4 miles of the track to the east of the village; Cheddington station wasn't staffed over the twenty-four hours and closed after the last train in the evening until the start of the following day's travel. Overnight in the station something like £2 or £3 was kept and security was adequate bearing this in mind.

The Train

The train was known as the 'Glasgow to Euston Travelling Post Office' (TPO); sometimes called the 'Up' special (trains travelling towards London are referred to as 'Up' trains, those travelling away are 'Down') or the 'Up' postal. It travelled through the night originating, in part, in Glasgow, where it left at 6.50 p.m. on 7 August 1963. It stopped 28 miles south at Carstairs, where the original coaches were joined by others, and when it crossed the border and stopped at Carlisle, even more were added – these coaches had come down from the north-east of Scotland. Thereafter the train travelled south with no other coaches joining.

It was solely for post. No freight or passengers were carried. The train comprised twelve coaches hauled by a diesel engine manned by a driver and a fireman (in the days of steam engines the fireman had a more defined role and eventually the title 'second man' was adopted but 'fireman' was a term that was reluctant to die out). The only other railway employee on the train was the guard – who was usually in the rearmost coach, so the remainder of the men on the train were General Post Office (as it was then called) employees. The train was due to arrive at Euston station in London at 3.59 a.m. on 8 August.

To most railway travellers a journey is punctuated by a number of different things; the point at which the newspaper page is turned, or the passing of the major towns, or the point where the train always jolts to wake up the sleeping passenger. Occasionally trains pass changing landscapes where someone has run up to bowl or a new car has joined the acreage of its dismantled cousins. For railwaymen, it's different. Every stretch of track has some kind of name or reference, each signal its own personality: it's true that one green light is much the same as any other, but each signal gantry or pole has its own unique identity. Some bridges have names (some are famous) but others, mere numbers. But for the train crew and signalmen these areas are important: the track – or road as parlance would have it – is split into sections. Each section has a signalman to ensure the safe and speedy passage of the train. He knows the train is due and the signalman for the previous section will notify him that it's coming; if all is clear then his sets of signals can be set to safe to let the train through. The signals are of two identities – the 'distant' and the 'home' – and like anything else there is the possibility of a malfunction and there is a procedure to follow when this happens. Moving trains from one point to another means for the train crew, motion, and for the signalman, safety. And if there is a malfunction then the train crew and the signalmen talk.

For the signalmen and train crew to talk, one of the train crew has to leave the cab of the train and approach the signal pole or gantry, where there is a telephone to the signalman. There are times when a fault will make a signal show red, or danger, and the driver can't proceed. But if the signalman says the light is set to green then it highlights a fault in the system – the driver is given clearance to proceed and the signalman can report the fault.

If, though, the signals should be showing green but show red, and the reason is because of some kind of other intervention, cutting the phone wires to prevent the communications becomes a necessity. If, for example, one wanted to rob the TPO, then to rig signals to show red instead of green and cut the phone wires from the signal to the signalman would help in bringing the train to a standstill and, as importantly, isolate it.

So the robbery took place on the night run of 7/8 August 1963, at a section between Sears Crossing signal gantry and Bridego Bridge, about 2 miles south of Leighton Buzzard and about 38 miles from Euston.

The Attack

At just a few seconds past 3.00 a.m. an amber light was viewed. This was a distant signal and gave a message to the driver to proceed with caution as the next light signal might be red – this would be the home signal. The driver started to apply the brakes. The home signal did show red, so around 5 yards from the signal gantry the train drew to a halt. Far ahead the green light of the next section could be seen, but the train crew had to make contact with the signalman first, to obtain permission to proceed. So the door of the locomotive opened and a man descended the steps on the side of the locomotive to walk to the phone at the bottom of the signal gantry. It was at this point, at around 3.03 a.m., that the Great Train Robbery started.

The Aftermath

When it finished is another question. One can say there are points in the history of the crime where a line can be drawn – all done and dusted. But overall the crime has become something of a legend and so the word 'finished' might be misplaced. Three of the robbers were never convicted, neither was their own train driver, most of the money wasn't recovered and the legacy of misery and bad luck seemed to permeate.

The question is bound to arise that, with its age and the attention given by writers, film-makers and the like, what is there to say that is new? And one has to recognise that repackaging an old product doesn't change it, and sometimes its new appearance is quite obvious and fools no one. But there are parts of the story that haven't ever really been examined. It's widely accepted that the robbery was the epitome of good planning and swift, stealthy execution, but after the thieves left the railway and settled back into their hideout it remained an epitome – but of incompetence. It was almost as though two sets of people had been involved – and here a novel might fail on plausibility. As the robbers demonstrated their bungling, the police demonstrated their expertise. The robbers seemed to change in personality and so did the police; from the country force where one beat saw nine crimes in a whole year, enter the Flying Squad who were going to sweep up the robbers with one stroke of the brush.

Taking the view that no more convictions are likely, then the end could be said to be in sight. But if history has no beginning, then it's also unlikely to have an end. So where does one start to tell the tale of one of the biggest media stories of the post-war era? The media want us to accept, and there's no reason not to, that there were four main groups of people into and out of which characters would move. First there were the robbers, then the train and Post Office staff, then the police and the legal machinery, and finally the families.

As the story developed over the years so did science and technology, and it would be helpful to assess what one can now suggest in view of this.

Therefore if I take the robbers as the starting point, and include the fictitious names given to the three who got away, I can start with a background onto which I can place the picture of the robbery and then follow the events broadly over fifty years.

1
THE ROBBERS

There were fourteen men in the Buckinghamshire countryside who were the train robbers, and two other men joined them that night: the man brought in to drive the train the few hundred yards from where it was stopped and ambushed to where it was robbed, and his minder. In the background were the three men I refer to as the 'law team', whom I shall describe in a moment, and then two men who brought the information to the robbers, or some of the robbers, in the beginning.

This operation would need some funding, and it would help to identify where that money came from. The story some of the robbers gave when they came out of prison was a German connection, which was soon demonstrated as false, but this came from one of the better written of the accounts, by Piers Paul Read. Robbers were spenders but a contemporary writer, Peta Fordham, suggested crime was changing and so, therefore, were the criminals: gone were the days of the opportunist and the 'smash and grab'; numbered were the days of wages snatches – it was time to plan thoroughly before acting. This sentiment was echoed by DSupt Fewtrell, who was head of the CID in Buckinghamshire. He said,

> The casual days of the raiders who went in for immediate big spending are over.
>
> The stakes are higher, the organisation better ... the new model criminals have turned it into a business, quite often a very successful one. The villains ... have got away with record-breaking

amounts of money ... outstripped their American and Continental rivals, [and] in scenario and plot they have even outdistanced the television and film script writers.

*

What is now thought to have been the funding robbery for the train was the BOAC (forerunner of BA) wages snatch at Comet House at Heathrow Airport in November 1962. This netted the gang £62,000, which would have been enough for the outlay and enough to keep key members of the criminal gangs out of trouble and therefore prison, so that their part in the train robbery would be secure. As a measure of what DSupt Fewtrell said about the professionalism of the gangs, he said that there was no evidence to connect the airport robbery with the train robbery. But when one considers the professionalism of the robbers, then there was plenty.

In the airport robbery, they were to be called the 'Bowler Hat Gang' as they dressed in pin-striped City suits and wore bowler hats – these concealed stocking masks just above the hairline and with the pin-striped suits the gang were not incongruous in the building, nor were their umbrellas, which concealed coshes. The robbery was soon accomplished and, with the drivers they had, they were away quickly. Heathrow Airport was different in those days, or rather the security wasn't as intense as it now needs to be. The gang drove off with the booty to a point in the airport perimeter road where they could cut their way through a chain holding a padlock on a gate, and sped off to the safety of London. The cars were later abandoned (one belonged to a famous television actor of the time, Craig Stephens) and the bolt-cutters were left on the back seat. Leaving the bolt-cutters like this jeopardised the job, because when the police investigated they could trace them. They had been bought by Micky Ball, who was a crook of sorts but a good driver and so his role was as a getaway driver. He was identified by the ironmonger from whom the bolt-cutters were bought, who also noted the vehicle he got into, which was registered to Gordon Goody. With an expert to testify that the perimeter fence chain was cut with the recovered bolt-cutters, it looked grim. Micky pleaded guilty (got five years and departed the criminal world), and his plea of guilty compounded difficulties for Gordon. But Brian Field, who was a solicitor's managing clerk, sorted a few things out, such as bail and his defence. The other robbers on the airport job were either acquitted or the charges were dropped. But Gordon stood trial twice; the first time he nobbled a juror and escaped by the skin of his teeth, but the second time he pulled the evidence to pieces.

There was evidence that he'd been seen by a man who was travelling on the top deck of a bus, which was proved unreliable; Gordon took photos to prove the man couldn't have seen him where he said he'd seen him. The ironmonger who'd sold Micky Ball the bolt-cutters was questioned on the point of identification – and the point was made when Gordon brought in as a witness another man who looked like Micky. This sowed some seeds of doubt. During the fracas of the robbery, where some resistance had been put up by the couriers transporting the money, Gordon's hat had been knocked off and now was an exhibit for the prosecution. Some money went into the hands of a police officer and the hat was changed for a much bigger one. If the witness swore that the hat came from Gordon's head then his head and the hat's size would match – in court they didn't. Gordon made some unfortunate comments to the crestfallen prosecution as he left the court, which he would later regret. The police had been made to look foolish, but were to have their day.

The Bowler Hat Gang now had a lot of cash to invest in their next robbery.

*

Before bringing in the rest of the gang, I want to discuss the men I described above as the law team.

John Wheater was a forty-one-year-old solicitor with a practice in New Quebec Street, just round the corner from Marble Arch in London. He was an ineffectual soul who was not particularly good as a solicitor and even worse as a businessman. But he sounded as though he was a gentleman and had a good service record from the Army, where he had risen to the rank of Major during the war. Mr Wheater had enough confidence in his managing clerk to leave most of the criminal stuff to him. His managing clerk was Brian Field, twenty-eight, twice married and about as corrupt as they come. He was also intelligent, and the clients of Mr Wheater's firm became contacts for his extra-curricular activities. Leonard Denis Field was no relation but, fast-forwarding for a moment, Mr Wheater and Lennie Field were to become Brian Field's fall guys; more of this later.

Lennie Field was actually a merchant seaman and Brian got to know him through his brother, who'd just gone away for horse doping.

Brian knew some of London's more accomplished villains and had put work their way before. It was with him that the train robbery was said to have its origins; at any rate this was where it met London's criminal underworld. He had heard of large sums of money being transported around by train with little or no protection – and he had two men whom he wanted to introduce to two of the villains: Gordon Goody and Buster Edwards.

Douglas Gordon Goody was born in 1930 and was unmarried. He lived some of his life with his mother in Putney and was very attractive to the ladies. He liked nice food and expensive suits and wasn't out of place in the more fashionable areas of London. Ronald Christopher 'Buster' Edwards was thirty-two and married to June, with a young daughter – they'd also had a son who died just after birth. Buster loosely described himself as a 'nightclub proprietor' but his premises became a focal point for the more professional criminals in London. Buster and his partners wanted to close the club down as it was a distraction from his family life and the excessive drinking had brought its own problems with the family, his health and the law (this was five years or so before the breathalyser was introduced but nevertheless the police were hot on drink-drivers). Following a bungled robbery in the West Country, during which Buster had received a few injuries, and a crash on the way back to London which gave him even more, they trashed the nightclub and decorated it with Buster's blood to make it look as though there had been a fight with a rival gang, and claimed the insurance. Buster could then get some medical attention.

Gordon had received a call from Brian Field, so, after meeting him – in the Old Bailey of all places – went to his office with Buster the following day to discuss some work. Brian was the intermediary and took them to meet two other men: one was a nondescript middle-aged man and the other was to be described as the 'Ulsterman'. There was information about the movement of huge amounts of money on the railways, detailing how the money was sent from the provincial banks to London as surplus to their stock balances and occasionally as old money for incineration. The sums involved could be huge, running into several millions.

This wasn't the only 'bit of business' the gang was considering at the time and, like with the airport robbery, one can make the mistake of seeing the train robbery in isolation. Both Gordon and Buster had heard stories about big money movements on trains before, and had tried their hand at it. But they had only netted £700 or so and found that stopping trains through the communication cord wasn't reliable. They were quietly sceptical about another foray into the railways but they found there were no passengers on the mail trains anyway. However, it was worth a thought because Brian had been reliable before and the Ulsterman had seemed confident in his information. They thought they should discuss things with other members of their gang, and when they got to Buster's flat in Twickenham they called two of their colleagues, Bruce Reynolds and Charlie Wilson.

Bruce Richard Reynolds was a thirty-two-year-old veteran of much criminal activity, which had seen him sent to prison in the past. For most people prison sounds like a grim experience, but for a criminal it's an ideal place where bonds are formed and relationships grow. Bruce had intelligence, charm and wit, and for a thief who was to rewrite the record books, he had a huge imagination. Like Gordon, he was a man who oozed ability and took the life of a criminal as near to that of an artist as society could dare to let him.

Growing up, Bruce had a pal with bright-blue eyes who too had matured into a professional thief. He was both loyal and respected. His name was Charles Frederick Wilson, he was married to Pat and they had three daughters.

This was the core of the team that had previously come together to act on Charlie's information to do the airport job – again the product of 'someone in the know' about the movement of money making up wages. After the airport robbery the gang had driven from the airport to Norbury in North London, where some of Bruce's associates were waiting: James Edward (Jimmy) White, the veteran thief, paratrooper and now thieves' quartermaster; Harry Booth, a friend of Bruce's not on the train job; John Thomas Daly, Bruce's brother-in-law, who was on the train job; and Roy John James, the other driver from the airport job, who briefly enjoyed professional motor racing.

So when the possibility of the train robbery came along, the first question they asked themselves was: Is there enough 'muscle' to do the job?

Bruce, Buster, Gordon and Charlie took a trip to Euston station to see the TPO loaded to go north that night, and could see that a good bit of the load was going into the second coach, the High Value Package (HVP) coach. The job looked as though it was there for the taking.

They had a total of eight men to look at the job but already it was clear there were difficulties to overcome. Raiding the train at Euston was a possibility but the alarm could easily be raised and the business ruined. Besides, there might be police involved and that generally increased the sentence if caught. So that option was out, and so was any possibility of an ambush at any of the stations the train stopped at along the way. They knew stopping a train was no easy task, and there was also the fact that there were sixty or seventy men working on the train. The whole gang wanted the job done, and of course they wanted to maximise the take, the 'prize'. If the HVP coach was always the second coach and wasn't a sorting coach then there might not be too many men on it. So, they wondered, was it possible to split the first two coaches from the rest of the train and make off into the night with the diesel and two coaches? Bruce's answer to this was 'yes', but he didn't know 'how'.

So the best plan was to stop the train between stations, separate the engine and first two coaches from the rest of the train, remove them, rob them and disappear into the night.

Buster had a lot of friends, and he kept his eyes and ears open. On the grapevine he'd heard of a gang who did stop trains to rob them, and he knew enough about the gang to feel comfortable approaching them.

Thomas William Wisbey was thirty-three and lived with his wife Rene and their two daughters in Camberwell. He'd been working for a good while with Robert Alfred (Bob) Welch, who was a club proprietor whose home life was said to be complicated. Nevertheless Tommy and Bob oozed the London charm that had endeared them to Buster and vice versa, so when Buster heard they were working with the rather muscular Frank Munroe and the incongruous forty-one-year-old florist Roger John Cordrey, he had remembered the oddball complexion of the firm. They were known as the 'South Coast Raiders' and their history was of good growth and success over a fairly short period.

Another associate, James Hussey, was a giant of a man with a pleasing personality whose face lit up when he smiled. He liked to have a bit of cash in his pocket and a suit for cruising the snooker clubs and bars of South London.

Bob Welch lived with his wife, Pat, and they had no children. He was a big man and fiery when roused.

Roger was married and had three sons but had kept out of the criminal limelight for a number of years, teaming up with an older thief and with Frank as minder. Both Roger and Frank had found their third man was not quite up to speed and so they needed to expand their gang in another direction. Tommy Wisbey and Bob Welch provided the solution. Frank had known them for a while and so they joined the curious little Roger and giant Frank.

Jim Hussey was also close to Bob Welch, so he appeared well trusted and would use violence when the necessity presented itself. None of them were thugs, but dedicated thieves who only used violence to get at, and keep, their prize.

Roger Cordrey wasn't quite as curious as at first glance. He was older than his counterparts and had turned to crime to fund, or rather bail himself out of, mounting gambling debts. But for all of that Roger was the epitome of outward respectability and always had the good grace to turn away if a coshing was a necessity. Once the gang had hit a string of successful train raids, the police became interested. Roger had a visit from the police and was outraged; they could only have known of him through his and Frank's old associate, so Tommy, Bob, Frank and Roger paid him a visit.

In those days there was a strict 'us and them' policy between the villains and the police, though there was plenty of evidence of police corruption. There were few instances of 'grassing', and few people were willing to point the finger and say, 'He did this.' But the old associate admitted the police had visited him and that he had 'grassed' – but he begged for mercy and had a couple of hundred pounds in cash on him, which he offered them. They took it. Tommy, Bobby and Frank gave him a good stiff talking-to as Roger walked away.

Buster went to Bob Welch's club in Elephant and Castle, where he had arranged to meet Tommy. Even then, with Buster's network of associates and connections, he only knew they had a 'geezer who knows how to stop trains' and Buster wished to consult with him. Tommy was very much surprised that these rumours of their activities were so well known. He took Buster up to Bob's office, where Frank Munroe was also present.

It seems Tommy's associates were as surprised as he that these rumours were abounding. Buster's reputation kept any ill feeling at bay and they knew they could trust him. So after Tommy's surprise and Bob and Frank's raised eyebrows, the men discussed, albeit in outline, what Buster had in mind. Tommy, Bob and Frank were sufficiently reassured to lay down the ground rule that this 'specialist who could stop trains', if he existed, would make up his own mind about whether he should get involved or not. Such things were rare; joining a firm was only embarked on when one knew one could trust one's associates – prison was there for mistaken character references.

Tommy got to work as he could smell something big, and a couple of days later a meeting was arranged. Buster went to Waterloo station, where he met Tommy and Roger Cordrey. Buster outlined the train job and also another possible job, and Roger asked him questions to test the reliability of the information. Roger was satisfied, and his firm were to join in the robbery.

It was a bit of an unusual amalgamation but Buster was getting a train specialist and three other thieves who were not only big, but reliable too. Gordon was receptive to the idea, reminding the others of the prize. The firm was taking shape. But one of Bruce's closest friends was nervous about the growing team and felt his trust of the others was just not enough – purely through his lack of knowing them. One word in the wrong ear and the whole lot would be implicated; he felt there were too many weak links. So he left the team – when the job happened he'd disappeared abroad. The story was that he later turned to drink and finally died by taking his own life in the mid-1990s. He has been named as Harry Booth, so I'll stick with that.

Jim Hussey was also in the gang; he'd left prison in late 1962 and floated, but he was known and trusted.

*

As they surveyed the possible locations for the robbery it became apparent that they'd be looking for a venue close enough to London but far enough away; not somewhere people were likely to be, an embankment rather than a cutting – rolling mailbags downhill is easier than carrying them up. Roger needed a set of signals, and the gang needed a road.

Tommy and Buster drove out to the north of London but even though they found the railway line easily enough they couldn't find the other requisites. So when they returned to Buster's flat they got some large Ordnance Survey maps and, as proximity to London was important, they followed the track out of London as it went north. North of Tring they found what looked to be the ideal location – deserted, with a quiet minor road leading under a bridge with no houses nearby. But a thorough inspection was needed. Bruce joined Tommy and Buster to make the first survey and they found the bridge easily enough: No. 127, Bridego Bridge.

The line was on an embankment and as the embankment met the bridge a buttress wall had been built to retain it, at the foot of which was a gateway into which the lorry could be reversed to load. The plan was taking shape – the train on top of the embankment and the robbers moving the mailbags down and into a lorry reversed into a gateway at the bottom of the embankment adjacent to the retaining wall. What became labelled as the 'crime of the century' was remarkably simple in its complexion.

Bruce travelled out with Roger for his opinion on the railway traffic aspect. It was a good spot and there was a home signal about half a mile down the line, with its distant signal about 1,300 yards further down towards Leighton Buzzard. Roger thought he could stop the train at the home signal, but the problem was isolating the locomotive and first two coaches; the HVP coach being second, with only five or six men on board. To isolate the remainder of the train, with about another seventy men on board, would necessitate dividing the train at the home signal gantry and moving it the half mile or so to the bridge for the attack. Bruce set about planning and made a number of trips up to reconnoitre; he even filmed the scene for briefing sessions.

Another part of the planning was regular night-time trips to the venue to assess the running and punctuality of the 'Up' TPO. By day, the two men could survey the line and Roger could make his own plans; but he could only hope to take either the distant or home signal – when he was persuaded to delegate the distant signal, Buster and Bruce wondered if they might have figured out Roger's technique themselves.

The gang was a large one now, with fourteen members. Not so big that everyone would be falling over each other, but not so small that the odds might be against them:

Bruce Reynolds, who would be way down the track to identify the TPO and radio back when the (now) familiar pinpricks of windows came into view just as the train travelled through Leighton Buzzard.
John Daly, who was at the distant signal to change it from green to amber or caution.
Roger Cordrey, who waited on the gantry to turn the home signal from green or clear to red.
Buster Edwards, who co-ordinated this part of the plan and was positioned just slightly to the north of Bill Jennings.
Bill Jennings, who with Buster and Jimmy White was part of the team to uncouple the train to divide the first two coaches and engine from the rest of the train.
Jimmy White, who was also the quartermaster in charge of all the requisites, from batteries for Roger to arranging the acquisition of the getaway vehicles and the buying of sleeping bags, food, drink and more!
Roy James, whose real skill wouldn't be used, but he had spent a lot of time in the sidings of train depots in North London with Jimmy to perfect the uncoupling.
Alf Thomas, who was to 'look after' the train crew.
Bob Welch, who with Alf received David Whitby from Buster.

To the north of the line were:

Gordon Goody, who was in charge of the assault on the locomotive, a 'heavy'.
Charlie Wilson, who was another heavy with Gordon and company. Five big men against two unsuspecting crew members should have been adequate. Charlie had a pleasant manner; after Mr Mills's injury it was he and Tommy Wisbey who dressed Mr Mills's wound and told him, 'We didn't want to hurt you.'
Jim Hussey.

Tommy Wisbey.
Frank Munroe.

Those are the fourteen members of the gang who conspired and executed the Great Train Robbery.

Two other men were there with a special role. One, a man who Piers Paul Read called Stan Agate, was to drive the train from where it was stopped at Sears Crossing to Bridego Bridge. Stan had no experience with heavy main-line locomotives, though, and had worked as a shunter driver, so the braking system of the main-line trains would not have been too familiar to him, and although he probably knew about the vacuum braking system, he didn't think through what was needed to release the brakes. Consequently, the engine didn't move.

In his planning, Bruce had wondered about the real driver of the train – would the gang be able to plead, or reason, or threaten him into driving that last half a mile or so to the bridge? In the event the real driver, Mr Mills, did drive the train but it wasn't until the gang were in the cab that they discovered this. Discretion is the better part of valour; Mr Mills acted wisely.

But the niggling question for Bruce was, what if he wouldn't?

So the answer lay, or so he thought, with one of his old cronies, Ronald Biggs. Bruce approached him to see if the old train driver he knew, Stan Agate, could help. There was a good payment to be made to both for this but Ronnie saw the opportunity for easy money so wormed his way into the gang, much to their disquiet.

The gang didn't know Ronnie Biggs well enough to work with him, and the train driver would be a very weak link; in the hands of the police one could almost guarantee he would give a lot of information. The gang became aware of the inclusion of Ronnie Biggs and Stan Agate fairly late on in the plan, when it was too late to effectively do anything about it, but it was a worry as Stan had no idea how these men operated and he didn't seem to grasp the real reason for their later occupation of Leatherslade Farm.

It has been said that one or more of the gang, particularly when Stan couldn't drive the train, suggested he be killed – at least he couldn't tell a soul then. But this is not supported by anything recorded at the time or since. They were thieves and were not violent men by choice. In fact, when Roy James was digging a hole to bury some items, Stan thought it was a grave and became agitated; the gang quickly reassured him. Violence would be used if necessary but the appearance of five men who were largely built and muscular usually communicated the need for discretion, and thus violence was avoided. I'll return to this later when discussing the driver and his injuries.

2

THE ROBBERY

The TPO consisted of a diesel engine and twelve coaches: the first coach was for parcels, the second was the HVP coach and the rest were an assortment of sorting and transport coaches. A corridor ran from the rear to the second coach; TPO coach-connecting corridors were offset so that there was no access to the first coach, nor to the engine or drivers.

The HVP coach contained the packets originating from banks in Scotland and the North and was destined for London, for delivery to the head offices of the banks. Sorting of bags containing these packets into mailbags and sacks was carried out mainly by a postman higher grade (PHG) at the originating sorting office.

On the train were seventy-seven Post Office staff under the direction of an inspector and an assistant inspector. In charge of the HVP coach was a PHG and at the time of the robbery he was in that coach with the assistant inspector and three other PHGs. The inspector was in the fifth coach and the other Post Office staff were working in the other coaches of the train.

Night-time on the railway was when passengers and commuters were safely tucked up in bed and so many more freight workings drove into the night. Usually TPOs ran to schedule, and delays were unusual; they obeyed the normal traffic signals.

The TPO was made up of coaches collected on its journey to Euston. The engine and first five coaches left Glasgow at 6.50 p.m. and arrived at Carstairs at 7.32 p.m. It was joined by four coaches that had left Aberdeen at 3.30 p.m. and arrived at

Carstairs at 7.15 p.m. The train then left Carstairs at 7.45 p.m., arriving at Carlisle at 8.54 p.m. where three more coaches were added to the train.

At Carlisle the guard was relieved by Thomas Miller, sixty-one, who was then with the train until it was attacked.

The train left Carlisle at 9.04 p.m. and stopped at Preston at just about 11.00 p.m.; it moved on to Warrington, where it arrived just over half an hour later and left at 11.43 p.m. before getting to Crewe at 12.12 a.m. At 12.30 a.m. the train left Crewe with a fresh driver and fireman: Jack Mills, fifty-seven, and David Whitby, twenty-six, respectively. They then drove the train for the remainder of the journey, stopping at Tamworth just after 1.20 a.m., Rugby at just after 2.10 a.m. and finally passing through Bletchley at 2.53 a.m. The journey continued until, finally, at 3.03 a.m., the train stopped just before the Sears Crossing home signal because it showed red against it. It was there that the robbery took place.

The robbery took place over roughly half an hour and the exact timing isn't known, though a good approximation can be made.

The starting point of the robbery was when the train came into Bruce Reynolds' view. Bruce sent the message that the TPO was in sight to John Daly at the distant signal, also picked up by Roger at the home signal: 'This is it. This is it. This is it.'

John removed the bulb from the green aspect of the distant signal and fixed two crocodile clips. It was later found that the wires attached to the crocodile clips stretched across the tracks where they met at a switch – this had simply been flicked at the appropriate time. The distant signal was virtually on the trackside and was known as a dwarf signal, so operating it from a distance was necessary – or he might be seen.

Another 1,300 yards up the line, Roger fixed a glove over the green signal, obliterating it, and wired batteries to the red light. The red showed. He could leave this and descend to help with the unloading of the train, which pulled up and stopped a few yards away from him. The time the train halted was 3.03 a.m.

Roy and Bill sprang into action and uncoupled the train, which only took a few seconds.

Mr Frank Fuggle was the inspector in charge of the TPO from Carlisle to Euston. His base position in the train was the fifth coach, and during the journey, or shift, he would visit the various coaches. At the time of the robbery he was at his base position.

There were five Post Office staff in the HVP coach at the time of the robbery. They were:

Thomas Kett, a forty-nine-year-old assistant inspector. His main duty was to supervise the staff in the second to fourth coaches from Carlisle to Euston.
Frank Dewhurst, forty-nine, a PHG. He was working in the HVP coach from Carlisle to Euston, and had responsibility for the bags containing the packages.
Leslie Penn, thirty-seven, a PHG. He too was working in the HVP coach from Carlisle to Euston.
Joseph Ware, fifty-five, a PHG. He joined the train at Tamworth at about 1.30 a.m. and was employed in the fifth coach until just before 3.00 a.m., when he was instructed to report to the HVP coach.
John O'Connor, twenty, a PHG. He also joined the train at Tamworth at about 1.30 a.m. He was employed throughout the train sorting mail, but just a few minutes before the robbery he was instructed to report to the HVP coach.

The stretch of railway where the robbery occurred consists of four sets of tracks. The train was travelling on the 'Up' fast line, north to south. On the locomotive the driver's seat is on the left side of the engine, facing forward. At the home signal, the fireman, Mr Whitby, left his seat on the right, passed behind the driver and climbed down onto the tracks. He went to the telephone at the base of the signal gantry. Mr Mills later explained that Mr Whitby didn't wait the regulation three minutes before attempting contact with the signalman. On the track, Mr Whitby could see the distant signal in the next section of line was green, which suggested that the line was clear and that there was a fault in the signal, but when he tried to contact the signalman he found the wires were cut.

He saw a man between the second and third coaches and thought he was a postman. He went towards him and, as he passed the open cab door of the locomotive, shouted up to Mr Mills, 'I'll go and see what's wrong.'

Mr Whitby said to the man, 'What's wrong mate?' But the man either didn't hear him or made out he didn't hear him, and walked across the slow line towards the embankment. He beckoned Mr Whitby to follow him, and, thinking now by his attire that the man was a railwayman, Mr Whitby thought he was there to sort out the signal and the wire of the phone to the signalman. He didn't think there was anything out of the ordinary and followed the man to the top of the embankment. But suddenly the man grabbed his elbows and pushed him towards the embankment, which made him stumble and slide down to where he now saw two other men. One of the men took hold of Mr Whitby, covered his mouth while brandishing a cosh and hissed, 'If you shout I'll kill you.'

The terrified fireman said, 'All right mate, I am on your side.'

After a short while Mr Whitby realised that the man on the embankment, together with one of the two men who had grabbed him as he fell, was gone and now there was only one man with him. He was told to stand up and was walked to the locomotive.

In the cab, he saw five or six masked men. Someone turned him to face the back wall of the cab and he was told to put his arms behind his back. He felt someone fumbling with his left wrist and then he was pushed into the engine room. There he saw Mr Mills with blood on his head and a man standing behind him holding a cosh. This man told Mr Whitby to close his eyes and keep them closed.

The driver and fireman gave slightly different versions of the events, so this is roughly how Mr Mills remembered events.

Mr Mills stated that Mr Whitby returned to the foot of the steps up to the cab and told him the wires were cut and then walked away towards the rest of the train. He turned his head to follow his movements and saw two men coming from the embankment who he thought were linesmen dealing with the signal fault – this would be routine, and was a usual assumption. So Mr Mills turned to his controls to start building up the pressure, which would release the brakes, because he expected Mr Whitby back with the all-clear, as he too could see a green light far ahead. He turned to look over his left shoulder for his fireman but saw another man mounting the steps, and he had a cosh in his hand. Suddenly he knew this was out of the ordinary and, as he said, he 'grappled' with the man – as he was above him he nearly succeeded in stopping his advance into the cab but was then struck from behind by someone who had entered the cab from the door behind the fireman's seat on the other side of the cab. He fell to the floor and very soon the cab seemed full of men. Someone said, 'Don't look up or you'll get some more.'

This was as terrifying an ordeal as Mr Whitby had gone through and, like his colleague, he complied with the gang's orders. He was told to get up and keep his head down and was taken to the passageway into the engine room. Here he found Mr Whitby with a man.

It wasn't long after this that Mr Mills was pulled out of the passageway and forced across the cab into the driver's seat. He was told to keep his head bent forward but he was to drive the train, slowly. He made ready to go but the vacuum controlling the brakes was not as it should be, so he rectified this before he could move forward. The tension in the cab settled slightly as they moved; Mr Mills guessed the vacuum had drained because some of the train had been separated from the rest, and the vacuum pipe wasn't properly resealed. Mr Mills moved the train, or rather the locomotive and the first two coaches, forward for what he thought was about half a mile, but actually the distance was about 1,200 yards. The order to stop from the gang member was not quite definite, but after receiving instructions – 'Stop. No. Go forward a bit more. Stop.' – he applied the brakes fully and was taken from his seat back into the corridor, where he was then handcuffed to Mr Whitby.

When asked later what they would do if Mr Mills didn't stop the train as instructed, it became clear this hadn't been thought about.

The train crew actually gave what the police described as reconcilable statements, and only one gang member could have been identified, that being the man Mr Whitby saw between the coaches after he had discovered the phone wires were cut. He was unable to identify a mugshot later, though. Mr Mills said they all wore boiler suits and balaclava-type helmets.

The gang was intent on bringing the train and Post Office staff together, so as the HVPs were removed Mr Mills and Mr Whitby were taken to the embankment and laid face-down. Mr Whitby didn't close his eyes and saw they were on a bridge over a road and the gang was in chain formation and loading what looked like an ex-Army lorry. They were sat down on the embankment for a few minutes while the gang took what they could before being taken to the rear of the HVP coach, where they climbed up to join the five Post Office staff who were all lying face-down in the carriage. Climbing onto the carriage was difficult as they were still handcuffed.

The assistant inspector in the HVP coach said that shortly after stopping, the train began to move and he heard steam escaping from the rear of his coach and he thought that the coupling between the coaches had been broken. Someone pulled the communication cord and others shouted through the windows at the driver.

All doors and windows of the HVP coach that could be closed were closed and locked; the corridor door of the HVP coach could only be locked by a special key that they didn't have. The train moved slowly forward and stopped again. A window of the coach was smashed in, so Mr Kett shouted to the others that it was a raid and they began piling mailbags against the doors as a barricade and other doors were bolted. Someone outside shouted, 'They're barricading the doors. Get the guns.'

Another window was smashed and two men climbed in and another man entered through the rear gangway door, one of them waving an axe. Within seconds, six to eight men were in the coach and Mr Kett and his colleagues could hear others shouting outside. All the Post Office staff were herded into the front of the coach and made to lie down. One man stood guard, making them keep their heads down and eyes closed.

The Post Office staff heard the sound of mailbags being unloaded. Soon they saw the driver and fireman come into the back of the coach and noticed the driver was injured. The gang told them not to move for half an hour, so they didn't, but as soon as things appeared quiet, two of the Post Office staff left the coach and walked back towards the rest of the train. None could identify their attackers.

In the third coach were other Post Office staff, including Stanley Hall and Dennis Jeffries.

When the train stopped at Sears Crossing, Mr Hall opened the door and saw a man standing between his coach and the HVP coach. After a few seconds, he saw another man come from under the joining bellows of the two coaches. One spoke to the other and they both walked away towards the engine. Mr Hall thought the men were railwaymen, so he closed the door and walked through his coach towards the HVP coach, but as he did so he saw it move away and the steam heating pipe burst, so his vision was impaired by steam. When the steam cleared, he saw that the HVP coach was drawing further away and one of the Post Office staff inside it was closing the door. He still didn't realise anything was wrong, but he saw the signal was red. His later recollection of both men he saw on the track was no more than the railway overalls they wore.

Mr Jeffries joined the train at Crewe and he was in the coach with Mr Hall when the train stopped. He looked out of the door and in the darkness could just make out two figures standing at the side of the track near the couplings with the HVP coach.

3

AFTERMATH AT THE TRACKSIDE

The guard, Mr Miller, was in his compartment at the rear of the train. When the train stopped he noted the time as 3.03 a.m. About two minutes later he heard the brakes of the train go on; the brakes of the train were controlled by a lever in the locomotive. The vacuum gauge in Mr Miller's compartment dropped to zero.

He didn't feel uneasy about things, but they were slightly out of the ordinary. He left his compartment and when he reached the ninth coach he spoke to Mr Fuggle.

Time passed, and Mr Miller began to think that they had stopped for a longer time than usual, so he decided to look out on the track, so climbed down to the trackside. He looked towards the front of the train but from where he was he couldn't see the locomotive. At this point the track is straight; he walked towards the front of the train and didn't see any rail or Post Office staff – he only thought he might see the fireman. When he got to the front of the train he found the locomotive and two front coaches were gone. He could neither see the locomotive nor hear it. He climbed back up into the train.

Back at the ninth coach, Mr Miller asked the Post Office staff to apply the handbrake; he went back to his compartment to prepare the track behind the train for any further traffic to make emergency stops lest a collision occur. This was done by placing detonators on the track at intervals of a quarter, a half and a mile. After this Mr Miller returned to the Sears Crossing telephone point but couldn't contact the signalman as the wires were cut.

At this point he began to feel as though something untoward had occurred.

The nearest station was Cheddington, and he knew they hadn't gone through it, so he thought he should go there to try and get help. But between the abandoned portion of the train and Cheddington he discovered the engine and front two coaches stationary and quiet at Bridego Bridge.

Mr Miller was surprised to find the side door of the HVP coach was open so he climbed up into it. Inside the coach he found Mr Mills and Mr Whitby sitting on some bags, still handcuffed together. He noticed the injuries to Mr Mills. He also saw three of the Post Office staff in the coach. They told him of the robbery and so he then set off towards Cheddington station to seek assistance. He stopped a train which was coming towards him, told the guard of the robbery and asked the crew to stop at the abandoned diesel engine and attend to it, which they did by driving it into Cheddington station.

At Cheddington signal box he could call for assistance. He recorded his time of arrival there as 4.15 a.m.

Referring back to the scene in the HVP coach for a moment, Mr Miller didn't see Mr Kett or Mr Penn, who had gone to try and summon help. Mr Kett thought they had seen the guard but this turned out to be a fireman for a train which had stopped to give help. The confusion was cleared up later by the police, who would, as a matter of course, investigate thoroughly any discrepancies in the statements. Even the most junior and inexperienced of policemen would consider anyone with access to the train that night as a suspect.

Thomas Windebank, a fifty-seven-year-old signalman, was on duty at Leighton Buzzard No. 1 signal box. At 2.58 a.m. he saw the TPO pass. At 3 a.m. he received an indication on a buzzer in his box that the signal lights at the distant signal at Sears Crossing were out. He assumed it was a signal failure and took no action; he waited for a telephone call from the fireman on the TPO. He didn't receive a call and at 3.10 a.m. the signalman from Cheddington signal box telephoned him to ask where the TPO was. Mr Windebank told him that the train had entered his section and explained what he thought was the signal failure. At 3.15 a.m. he noticed that the train had passed the signals at Sears Crossing – he wouldn't be able to tell it was only a part of the train but his indicator showed the approach line to Sears Crossing as being 'still engaged', so a train was still in that section. It was then he thought that part of the train had been left behind or, more likely, that there was a track failure. He arranged for a linesman to be called out to check the line and then advised the Control Office at Euston, and the signalman at Cheddington box. It was his intention to ask the driver of the next 'Up' train to examine the line and report the position of the TPO at Cheddington. He later spoke to the driver of the next train, and discovered the TPO had been robbed.

Mr Frank Mead was a signal technician and he arrived at Sears Crossing at 4.45 a.m. He found all four signal box telephone wires had been cut and the home signal had been interfered with. He saw four dry-cell batteries connected by wires to the red bulb with a switch in between. The green light was covered by a man's glove. This would block the green on the signal until the switch was thrown, when a red light would appear. When he examined the signal, the red light was showing.

Mr Eric Sidebottom was an assistant linesman and he arrived at Sears Crossing at 5.10 a.m. to assist Mr Mead with the repairs. He examined the distant signal and found the bulb missing from the green and found an electric lead with two crocodile clips attached. He saw that the lead went across one set of rails and that it lay on the rails but had been cut by a passing train. Mr Sidebottom didn't find any batteries but thought that the same method was used to show a caution signal on the distant as had been used to cause a stop signal on the home. The difference was that the bulb had been removed from the green.

Mr Mills and Mr Whitby were taken to the Royal Bucks Hospital, Aylesbury, where Mr Mills was examined and treated by the Senior House Surgeon, Dr Syed Masud. He had a number of lacerations to the head and needed fourteen stitches. He was detained for observation and left for home on Saturday 10

August. He travelled with his wife, who had come down from Crewe.

Medical treatment was not necessary for Mr Whitby or the Post Office staff.

The clothing Mr Mills had worn that night was collected from his home on 12 August and sent for scientific analysis. A blood sample was also taken.

4

THE ESCAPE

The gang was successful in delaying any information getting to the police. As the locomotive with the first two coaches pulled away and steam escaped from the pipes, the Post Office staff realised the train had parted and rushed to Mr Fuggle as the inspector in charge of the train to report the event. He was later to say that he sent his men out into the Buckinghamshire countryside as the raid had started, but this has to be treated with some scepticism – all they knew at this point was that the locomotive and first two coaches were gone and the train had parted.

From the time the train was stopped at Sears Crossing at 3.03 a.m. and the thieves leaving Bridego Bridge about half an hour or so later, it wasn't until about 4.25 a.m. that a message from Cheddington signal box reached the Bucks Police HQ at Aylesbury, and then it had gone through Euston and New Scotland Yard. On the other hand, one has to consider what the message actually was. One report simply says a theft had occurred – Cheddington was closed at night with only a few pounds on the premises, so one can understand the slowness of response. The first police car is recorded as arriving at Cheddington at 4.36 a.m.

*

The probable route taken by the gang from the scene of the robbery to Leatherslade Farm was reconstructed by the police from information gleaned from witnesses: it was over almost wholly 'C' roads and countryside. Three points on the route cross over 'A' roads, which the gang might have thought of as danger points. The police would have been unable to intercept the gang's convoy unless there had been earlier information. This is from the official police record:

> Leaving Bridego Bridge travelling westwards following 'C' roads Nos 49 and 37 through Ledburn via C.75 and 76 to Wing when the A.418 Aylesbury to Leighton Buzzard road is crossed. Then via C.8 and 71 to Cublington and Whitchurch where the A.413 is crossed but staggered so 300 yards are travelled until the gang picked up the C.57 via Oving and Pitchcott and then on to Quainton and Kingswood by C.25, 30, 75 and 112 where the A.41 is crossed. The C.3 and C.60 then to Brill and the B.4011 Thame Road where Leatherslade Farm entrance is within 200 yards.

So the route was completely rural and to the north of Aylesbury, travelling from east to west.

The gang were using two Land Rovers and a 5-ton truck, travelling in convoy. They had a transistor radio on which they heard the first message transmitted by Bucks Police at 4.28 a.m. At this time they would have been back at Leatherslade Farm. This was an approximation considering the gang took about an hour to make the journey. Overall the route covered 28 miles and in daylight the police re-enacted the journey and, at speeds of 35–50 mph, took forty-eight minutes.

5
REPORTING THE CRIME

The first report to the police was to New Scotland Yard at 4.24 a.m. It was a message from the Control Office, Euston station, who had received a call from the signal box requesting police and an ambulance to a robbery and break-in at Cheddington station. This request was relayed at 4.25 a.m. to Bucks Police HQ at Aylesbury and they alerted two local cars and instructed them to attend the scene.

The railway station at Cheddington was fairly new, but small and in a rural area. If anything, sending two cars to the scene was a good and quick response by the police and adequate for a break-in at the station; quite in keeping with what one might expect with the information they had.

*

Once the staff on the main part of the train were alerted that a robbery had occurred, they sent men to get help. However, it isn't certain when the actual situation was realised. One report said the men in the third coach rushed to the inspector in charge of the train as the first two coaches were moving off, and he sent men to get help at once. But it wasn't until the front two coaches and the locomotive were found – or, more to the point, the railway and Post Office staff were found – that the story unfolded.

At Sears Crossing, all of the surrounding houses had their phone lines cut. One of the men found Redborough Farm and roused the occupier; he borrowed a bicycle to get him to Linslade police station, a distance of 3 miles. In the meantime, the alarm had been raised from Cheddington.

*

The first of the patrol cars, with police constables Arthur Atkins and Douglas Milne, arrived at Cheddington station at 4.36 a.m. There was then quite a dramatic change as the real situation became known.

By now the man on the bicycle had arrived at Linslade police station, where Inspector James Mellows lived – he was the first of the senior police officers to arrive at Sears Crossing and he recorded the finding of the rear portion of the train. At 5.08 a.m., he contacted Bucks Police HQ at Aylesbury by radio to seek assistance, telling the control room there of the robbery and what assistance he wanted; he referred perhaps to all of the senior officers of Bucks Police: 'Turn the lot out.'

He wanted the CID, but his training and experience hadn't prepared him for this.

In the meantime PCs Atkins and Milne remained at Cheddington station to act as an incident post. Their shift ended at 8.00 a.m. And, like other night workers, they retired to bed. In the afternoon, when they awoke and saw the evening newspapers, they were staggered at the value of what had been stolen.

6

POLICE ACTION

At 4.36 a.m., when the true situation became known, DSupt Fewtrell and Assistant Chief Constable George Wilkinson were telephoned. DSupt Fewtrell arrived at Bucks Police HQ at around 4.50 a.m. and the ACC at 5.30 a.m.

A police constable had been sent to the Royal Bucks Hospital with a handcuff key to try and release the driver and fireman of the train, who were still handcuffed together.

The ACC and DSupt Fewtrell left for the scene of the crime at about 5.30 a.m. Detective Sergeant George Gaunt of the Bucks Police Photography and Fingerprint Department, and Detective Sergeant Philip Fairweather of the Aylesbury Division CID were also to attend. Detective Constable John Bailey, also of the Photography and Fingerprint Department, received a call as well.

The Scene

Sunrise was recorded at 5.33 a.m. that Thursday morning, and the weather was dry and mild. The scene of crime in its entirety covered 4 miles. Inspector Mellows appears to have quickly appreciated the position and was soon aware that a considerable amount of money had been stolen. Following up the line from Redborough, he found the locomotive and the first two coaches. He saw various exhibits along the line and made a note of them and their positions for later reference to the CID. Inspector Mellows, in passing his messages to Bucks Police HQ, had asked that, in addition to the attendance of senior officers, roadblocks should be set up around the area, and neighbouring police stations informed. He also asked for dogs and handlers. Inspector Mellows made arrangements for isolated local places to be searched and he patrolled the lanes on both sides of the tracks.

Local beat officers arriving to assist were despatched to patrol the surrounding district.

The first CID officer, DS Fairweather, arrived at the scene at about 5.10 a.m. and wasted no time in starting to make enquiries generally of the railway and Post Office staff. He saw the ACC and DSupt at the scene at around 6.00 a.m. They left again around 7.30 a.m.

DS Gaunt and DC Bailey of the Photography and Fingerprint Department arrived at the scene at 6.30 a.m. and started work on the attacked portion of the train, which had been put onto the Aylesbury loop line at Cheddington. This was a big task and they were called to Sears Crossing signal gantry, where they examined the signals and batteries used by the thieves and took photographs before returning to the task at Cheddington. DS Gaunt was later informed by DSupt Fewtrell that New Scotland Yard were going to be called in and that he was to take all the necessary photographs of the engine, train, station, Bridego Bridge, signals and other evidence left on the tracks.

It was some time after 10 a.m. that DS Fairweather saw DSupt Fewtrell, who was then showing the chief constable the scene.

7

THE INVESTIGATION STARTS: 8–13 AUGUST

The first couple of days of the investigation started with the police simply not knowing where to look, but the time came when particular suspects came into view, and later a time when they could closely focus on them; this period can be discussed in three parts. The first part was the immediate aftermath of the raid; the second part was when their hideout at Leatherslade Farm was found; and the third involved what the evidence at the farm told them.

As far as the farm was concerned, the gang might just as well have left calling cards.

It's always been questioned whether the fingerprints said to have been found at the farm were actually found there. Well, they did satisfy the court, and if they hadn't and the men had been acquitted then the robbers could have gotten clean away. As it was, a number of the men didn't leave any fingerprints at the farm, including Gordon Goody; Roger Cordrey's were not found and, as has been widely accepted, neither were Bill Boal's. The robber's own train driver didn't leave fingerprints, and Ronnie Biggs, his minder, did. Overall, once the not guilty pleas had been rejected, the men who were said to have occupied the farm for the first four or five days have never convinced anyone they weren't there. So the discovery of the farm was a turning point.

Exhibits

Of course the farm and its contents were exhibits, but now we must backtrack.

When Bucks Police were first informed of a crime it was the report of a theft at Cheddington station, which hardly warranted, on the face of it, more than just a couple of men in a car to investigate. But it became clear as the morning of 8 August moved on that this was a crime of huge proportions and it wasn't for a while that the size of the enquiry was actually realised. As far as exhibits were concerned, their numbers grew and grew.

It was at the scene of the robbery that first morning that the 'collection' started and it was thought wise that one officer should be placed in charge of the collection, labelling and recording of exhibits.

Incident Room

To keep the enquiry separate from other police matters, an incident room was set up at Bucks Police HQ in Aylesbury.

The building itself was modern and hadn't long been commissioned so the new conference room was utilised at once. It had two telephone extensions and the GPO installed a further three lines from the switchboard and one was a direct line in.

At just after 10.30 on the morning of 8 August, a message was sent to New Scotland Yard and to the chief constables of all neighbouring police HQs. The message is quoted here in full:

> At approximately 02.45 hours today a mail train robbery occurred between Leighton Buzzard and Cheddington, Bucks. 120 mail bags containing a very considerable sum of money are missing.
>
> It is thought that persons responsible may have hidden up and attempt to get away by mingling with normal morning traffic. Observation and frequent spot checks of traffic vehicles is requested.

Meanwhile at Bucks Police HQ, the staff were busy dealing with messages received from the public as the robbery had already been reported on by the BBC.

At the time of the robbery, the fireman on the train, Mr Whitby, saw what he described as a 10-ton Army-type lorry (later amended to 5 tons). This matter will be referred to again, particularly in view of the following message received at Bucks Police HQ from the Linslade sub-division at 6 p.m. that evening:

> Re: Mail Robbery. About 1.20 a.m. 8th August 1963, three vehicles were seen on the Cublington–Aston Abbotts Road, travelling towards Aston Abbotts. All three vehicles were in close convoy. They are described as – a small vehicle, an Army-type lorry, large wheels exposed, and a light Land Rover.

Others

Liaison between the various bodies involved soon gained momentum. At about 8.30 a.m., Mr Clifford Osmond, who was Controller of the GPO Investigation Branch, phoned Brig Cheney at Bucks Police HQ. It was agreed a meeting should take place and this was arranged for 3.00 p.m. the same day. Mr Osmond was accompanied by members of his staff.

Brig Cheney contacted Commander George Hatherill at New Scotland Yard, asking for their presence at the meeting. DSupt Fewtrell attended the meeting with the chief constable. Commander Hatherill brought with him Detective Superintendent Gerald McArthur.

Brigadier Kenneth Holmes, Director Postal Services Department, General Post Office, attended with members of his staff.

Mr William Gay, Head of British Transport Police, and representatives of his staff also attended.

Brig Cheney and DSupt Fewtrell told the gathering of the information so far in their possession regarding the robbery and of the enquiries being conducted. Mr Osmond said that he believed the theft was in the region of £2.5 million pounds.

At the conclusion of the meeting Commander Hatherill told Brig Cheney that DSupt McArthur would be sent straight up to Aylesbury to assist in the enquiries. Detective Sergeant (John) Jack Pritchard would be with him. They arrived in Aylesbury that evening.

At Bucks Police HQ, DSupt McArthur and DS Pritchard were briefed of the enquiries made and actions taken. They arranged for road checks to be made the following morning for two hours, commencing an hour before the time of the robbery to one hour after. It was hoped that this would find regular travellers at this hour who might have seen something.

They also talked with farmers in the area surrounding the scene of the robbery. Deserted farms and outbuildings, ex-RAF and Army camps likely to be used by the thieves as a hideout were pointed out to them.

DSupt Fewtrell sent another message out to neighbouring Police HQs.

> Ref: railway robbery.
>
> Bearing in mind possibility that the stolen mailbags might still be concealed within a reasonable distance of Cheddington, would you please continue the searches you have already organised of derelict farm buildings barns, disused railway bridges, canal barges and other likely places. In addition to mailbags we are interested in a 10-ton Army lorry and a light blue or grey long wheel base Land Rover with hard top. One of these vehicles may have a broken wing mirror.

On Friday 9 August, DSupt McArthur, DS Pritchard and DS Fairweather discussed the steps already taken and those which were needed next. The threat to the men left in the HVP coach that someone would be watching it for thirty minutes was discussed. It was thought possible that the gang needed thirty minutes to get back to their hideout, so the detectives thought they might be within 15 to 30 miles of the crime scene.

Searching such a vast area even with help was not practical. On the other hand there was always the thieves' belief that the long arm of the law was about to grab them, so tensions might be running a little high, despite being surrounded by tons of banknotes. So the detectives decided to announce their belief that the gang had a hideout within 30 miles of the crime in the hope that it would disturb any feeling of comfort the gang might have had.

Their announcement was made at a press conference on 9 August (this appeared as a second feature in the *London Evening*

Standard on 10 August), but road blocks were not set up.

DSupt McArthur and DSupt Fewtrell left Bucks Police HQ and went to examine the scene; strangely they found that the locomotive and the first (parcels) coach had been removed.

Detective Superintendent Maurice Ray of the Fingerprint Branch at New Scotland Yard was coming out to examine the locomotive and coaches, and enquiries were commenced to trace them. Meantime, DSupt Ray started work on the HVP coach which had been left for him. The parcels van was traced to Windermere and the engine to Crewe. These were returned to Cheddington on Saturday 10 August.

DSupt Fewtrell had left clear instructions that the locomotive and coaches should be left at Cheddington. It transpired that Detective Superintendent Francis Ward of the British Transport Police had been 'anxious to get the diesel engine and parcels van back into service'.

He apparently spoke to DS Fairweather about this and the bizarre decision was made to release these two key items of evidence. DSupt Ward and DS Fairweather should have known better.

8
LEATHERSLADE FARM

DSupt McArthur met with representatives of the Criminal Intelligence Department who came out to Aylesbury on 11 August. Word from the grapevine had told them the gang had thought they would need a twenty-minute time span to reach a hideout, which was a farm believed to be owned by a horse dealer somewhere on the outskirts of Aylesbury. They had received information about Bob Welch, who was, it turned out, involved, and they put his house – and associates (not named) – under surveillance.

Detective Superintendent John Cummings later said there was an informant from the underworld he was in touch with. He also said the informant was reliable. The twenty-minute time span and the horse dealer's farm weren't at all reliable. Bob Welch and his associates may have simply been an educated guess as with Tommy, Frank and Roger he had robbed trains, or so Buster Edwards had told them he'd heard; so was this simply underworld rumour or genuine information? Also, Roger Cordrey had a visit from the police because of information from his old associate. The source of DSupt Cummings's information, if what he said years later was true, was a villain with his own gang. It seems doubtful that DSupt Cummings's information was genuine; it was a train robbery so the question was, who was, or had been, robbing trains? And what gang was ambitious enough and organised enough to be considered?

But DSupt Cummings encouraged the search to focus on a horse dealer in Aylesbury, about 10 miles to the west of where the sixteen men were holed up in a farm right off the beaten track. It couldn't be seen from the road and was a comfortable (as the gang thought) distance from the scene of the robbery.

To give some background to the place, it is only 2 miles from the Oxfordshire border and is in the parish of Oakley.

In August 1963 the farm was empty. The previous owner, Bernard Rixon, had moved with his family to Dunsdon, outside of Reading in Berkshire. He'd bought the farm in July 1952 and lived there until 7 July 1963. The house was put up for sale in the spring of 1963 and among other agents looking for a buyer was Midland Mart, of Bicester, Oxfordshire.

Towards the end of May 1963 Mr Rixon received a telephone call from John Wheater, saying he had a client who wished to buy the property and who would pay the money immediately in cash. Mr Rixon was led to believe that one of two men who had called at the farm a day or two earlier was a prospective purchaser and a member of Mr Wheater's staff.

Mr Rixon left the matter with his solicitor and a price of £5,550 was agreed on. Mr Rixon understood that a deposit of £555 (10 per cent) had been paid to the agents, Midland Mart. He agreed, on his solicitor's advice, that the buyer could get into the premises when the balance of the price was paid. But he was told there was a bit of a hold-up, and that full settlement couldn't be made until 13 August, because the purchaser's money would not be available until then. The buyer wanted access to the farm by 29 July 1963, and finally it was agreed he could take over on that date, providing he paid interest on the balance owing to cover the mortgage on the new property Mr Rixon was buying. This was agreed between his solicitor and Mr Wheater, acting on the behalf of who he thought was his client, Mr Leonard Denis Field. All of this was agreed and it doesn't seem as though Mr Wheater or Lennie Field knew, at this stage at any rate, that the purpose for the purchase, or near purchase, was to give the gang somewhere to hide.

Mr Rixon left the farm on Sunday 7 July but left his parents and the majority of the furniture in the house. His parents moved out on 29 July. Before leaving the house, Mr Rixon had a telephone call from a Mr Field asking him to leave the key. By arrangement this was left with a neighbour in Thame Road, Oakley.

The word 'farm' isn't an accurate description and the building was a cottage that had been added to over the years and by the early 1960s was suitable accommodation for two families living separately – Mr Rixon and his family lived in one part and his parents lived in the other. There were outbuildings that seemed, to any purchaser looking to conceal two Land Rovers and a 5-ton truck, to be ideal.

Altogether the farm was of 5 acres and it stood on a rise in the land where it looked down on the B6011, which was a road to Thame from Oxford, and it commanded good views of the countryside.

There was a track of about 300 yards leading to the place from the road and at the time of the robbery the foliage lining the track made it all but impossible to see from the road. This was the only entrance and the track was hard and robust but rough.

The gardens and land were not well kept and Mr Rixon used the outbuildings to store his collection of motorcycles and parts. His main occupation was not that of farmer; he was involved in the buying and selling of greengrocery. Mr Rixon was never seriously considered to have played any role in the conspiracy or in the robbing of the train.

Leatherslade Farm was not shown by name on the Ordnance Survey map; it was shown as Nuthooke Farm. It was known locally as 'Rixon's place', which is how even the local beat policeman knew it.

At the entrance to the track from the main road there was a barn and other buildings that housed a milking unit. These were owned by a local farmer and were generally run on his behalf by Mr John Maris, a cowman.

It seemed to be fairly well known locally that Mr Rixon wished to sell the property.

9

THE INVESTIGATION CONTINUES: 8–13 AUGUST

Following the initial conference of 8 August, in the afternoon of 9 August another conference was held at Bucks Police HQ with officers of the British Transport Police and members of the GPO Investigation Branch. Information was pooled and it was decided who would deal with what aspect of the enquiry. The GPO investigating officers were to take statements from the Post Office staff, other than those in the HVP coach, from whom statements had already been taken, and the British Transport Police were to seek out as much information as they could from their staff employed on the line.

In the meantime a message had been circulated on behalf of British Railways as to future action to be taken by railway staff should a TPO be delayed in any section between signal boxes.

*

The pond alongside Bridego Bridge was fished by around 180 members of the Berkhamsted Angling Society. Each was seen by the police to find out if any member of the gang, under the guise of an angler, had fished or pretended to while watching movements on the railway track. This didn't produce any helpful information.

*

DSupts McArthur and Fewtrell and DSs Pritchard and Fairweather spent time studying maps and deciding which particular farms and smallholdings should be searched. This was not an easy task as the county, especially around Aylesbury, was agricultural with a good many farms and smallholdings. The question of using servicemen from local camps to assist searches was considered, but for this search the police thought they could rely on their own staff.

At 9 a.m. on Sunday 11 August about eighty uniformed and CID personnel drawn from Bucks and Hertfordshire (Herts) Police reported at Bucks Police HQ, where they were briefed. Thirteen likely premises had been selected as possible hideouts and these were all searched – search warrants had been issued.

By midday the searches were finished but nothing helpful was found. Suggestions were made for other searches, which again were not fruitful.

The thought occurred to DSupt Fewtrell that the thieves might start thinking about moving from their hideout so he circulated the following message on the evening of 11 August: 'Attention of all foot and mobile patrols is drawn to the fact that the money may be moved at night either in bulk or in part.'

The searches continued but with the size of the area it was daunting. The thought of encountering a large group of men was also considered, so the police officers worked in teams of five.

On the afternoon of Monday 12 August DSupt Fewtrell attended a conference at Herts Police HQ. It was here that it occurred to the investigating team that local farms or cottages which may have been recently sold or let would be worth looking into. DSupt Fewtrell circulated the Herts Police, Bedford (Beds) Police and Northampton (Northants) Police as well as sending the brief to his own team. It read,

> Reference to Mail Robbery
>
> Bearing in mind that premises might have been specifically purchased or rented for use for the immediate concealment of the stolen property and its transport, please have enquiries made of Estate Agents and obtain information of transactions during

> the past six months involving likely premises within 30 miles of Cheddington, particularly farms, derelict houses etc. Please follow up where appropriate.

But on 13 August, Leatherslade Farm was discovered. Two of the teams organised to make searches on this day were disbanded while the team under the Aylesbury sergeant was diverted to Leatherslade Farm.

10
OTHER FORCES

The Flying Squad

Detective Inspector Reginald Roberts was called in from Essex, where he'd been sent to deal with a case, and was briefed to look after enquiries for the Metropolitan Police in relation to the train robbery. He set up an incident room at New Scotland Yard and although he gave some matters personal attention, he mainly fed things through to the Flying Squad. As time went by at least eighteen Flying Squad officers, and often as many as thirty, were working on the train robbery. There was daily liaison with Detective Chief Superintendent Ernest Millen, who had directed that priority was given to the train robbery case.

Herts Police

On Sunday 11 August an inspector, two sergeants and eight constables went to Aylesbury for briefing with the Sunday searches of farms. They searched a farm near Tring, and were assisted by RAF Police.

On 12 August DSupt Fewtrell attended a conference at Hatfield that detailed plans to search the Herts/Bucks boundary, which wasn't far from Cheddington.

Because the police had the breakthrough on 13 August of finding Leatherslade Farm, all searches were stopped.

Beds Police

In Bedfordshire, after the first information from Bucks Police HQ, road checks were held at Ampthill and on the A5. Patrolling vehicles and divisions were informed. At 4.52 a.m. on 8 August, a further message from Aylesbury explained fully the nature of the robbery, and all divisions were then asked to put on road checks.

On 10 August, following a phone call between DSupt Fewtrell and his opposite number in Beds Police, a memorandum was sent out from Beds Police HQ for searches to be made of derelict farm buildings, farms, disused railway buildings and other isolated buildings in the county. Beat officers were asked to seek the co-operation of farmers in finding farm premises that had recently been let.

A second memo to the Beds Police on 12 August extended the search, which was again extended on 13 August.

Oxfordshire (Oxon) Police

This county boundary is only a short distance from Leatherslade Farm.

The head of Oxford CID offered uniformed and CID personnel. Searches were made of derelict and unused buildings and these were reported on.

*

The first time that Leatherslade Farm was brought to the notice of the police as being a possible hideout for the thieves was late on Sunday 11 August, when a detective inspector from Oxon CID saw an informant in an Oxford club. It was thought that 'Rixon's place' at Oakley was a likely spot as a hideout for the thieves as it was isolated and little known. The informant said he knew Mr Rixon because they were both interested in motorcycles, and he knew the farm was up for sale. The informant said it was just a hunch but as far as he was aware the farm hadn't been sold up to a few days before the robbery.

The following day the officer made some more enquiries, mainly to verify some of the information he'd been given, and he thought there might be something in it. As Mr Rixon was now living at the sub post office at Dunsden, Berkshire, he phoned Aylesbury and left a message:

> Whilst making enquiries at Wheatley, Oxfordshire, re mail robbery, information was received that the premises at Leatherslade Farm, Brill, Bucks, were on the market for some time with no prospective purchaser. These premises were purchased a few weeks ago for a large sum of money. The informant suggested that this may be of interest to the robbery.

On the morning of 12 August, Police Constable Peter Collins was on duty in the incident room at Aylesbury when he received a phone call from Mr John Alfred Maris, who worked on a farm in Oakley. He said he was suspicious that Leatherslade Farm may have been the hideout of the train robbery gang. This information was passed on to DSupt Fewtrell.

Later that day, Mr Maris saw in the paper that police were interested in isolated farms as they thought that the robbers may be using one. He knew Mr Rixon had left so he went up to the farm to have a look around. He found that the curtains were all drawn and that a large lorry was parked in one of the outbuildings.

At 9.05 a.m. on 13 August, Sergeant Ronald Blackman of Waddesdon received a message from Bucks Police HQ that Leatherslade Farm had been sold recently, and he was asked to have a look around the place. Sgt Blackman had never heard of Leatherslade Farm and contacted Police Constable John Woolley of Brill, and another police constable who had worked the Brill beat. Neither of those two knew Leatherslade Farm either, but PC Woolley thought it meant a farm at Oakley that everyone called 'Rixon's place'. As these discussions were taking place, Mr Maris made another call to the Bucks Police HQ. Sgt Blackman met PC Woolley at 10.30 a.m. and they went to Leatherslade Farm together. They met with Mr Maris and then examined the farm. The two officers went into the main building and were struck by what they found. There was a huge amount of food and provisions. Upstairs there were sleeping bags and bedding, which suggested a number of people had been to the farm. When they searched the basement cellar they found the mailbags that confirmed that the gang had used the farm. Sgt Blackman telephoned Bucks Police HQ at 11.33 a.m. and then returned to the farm.

11

ACTION AT THE FARM

At the time Sgt Blackman telephoned the Bucks Police HQ, Comdr Hatherill and DCS Millen were at Aylesbury. They had spent two hours that morning meeting with DSupts McArthur and Fewtrell and later with Brig Cheney. In view of the weight of work the enquiry had created, it was decided that more Metropolitan Police officers were needed. That afternoon five more officers arrived at Aylesbury.

When the information was received at Bucks Police HQ, the brass both from Bucks and New Scotland Yard went straight out to the farm.

The first job was for the farm to be closely guarded until the fingerprint and forensic laboratory staff had examined the place. One of the search teams was directed to Leatherslade Farm for guard duties. An incident room was set up at Brill police station and remained there from 13 to 16 August.

On 14 August a public address system was used on a police car, and this toured seventeen local villages.

It was of no surprise that as soon as news of the discovery of the farm was announced, the media descended in force. But rather than exclude the media, it was partly in the police's interest to liaise with them to publicise as far as they could that the farm had been discovered – the gang would then know it wasn't a bluff.

*

Mrs Emma Nappin lived with her husband, Arthur, and their home faced the Thame Road and Leatherslade Farm: the farm is about half a mile away. She went to bed at about 10 p.m. on 7 August but she awoke around midnight and as she couldn't sleep; she got up and walked to the window. She saw a bright light on a vehicle in Thame Road. As it approached the Brill Road, the light was dimmed. She then noticed a solo motorcycle, a covered van and another motor vehicle had turned right into Brill Road. They passed in front of her house. She didn't take too much notice at the time and went back to bed. But she woke again at about 4.00 a.m. and was again restless. She got up, and at about 4.30 a.m. she heard the sound of vehicles. She went to the window as she'd done earlier and saw a solo motorcycle, a covered van and another vehicle coming from the direction of Brill. She was fairly sure they were the same vehicles she'd seen earlier. They passed the front of her house and turned into Thame Road, in the direction of Leatherslade Farm. They were showing only very dim lights and she then lost sight of them.

*

On 14 August DSupt Ray, two inspectors and a photographer started their examination of Leatherslade Farm. They were there for three days, and collected over 200 crime-scene photographs, over 350 fingerprint and palm-print photographs and also removed over 1,500 bank envelopes that they would examine.

Then the forensic team moved in. They also examined the farm for three days under the direction of Dr Ian Holden, who returned a fortnight later to re-examine some evidence.

A couple of little-known branches of the Metropolitan Police also attended the farm. Motor vehicle thefts were a speciality and in a short time the three vehicles found at the farm were identified and given a full history – two had been purchased and one stolen.

After the initial enquiries into the purchase of Leatherslade Farm had been made, mainly by DS Pritchard, all the documents were handed over to a specialist in fraud and conveyancing.

When PC Woolley first visited the farm on 13 August, he saw in one shed an Army-type lorry. It was partly covered with a green tarpaulin sheet, but he could see that although most of the vehicle was coloured khaki-green, the cab had been hand-painted yellow. In a locked garage he saw a Land Rover, and he saw another Land Rover in another garage some yards back down the driveway. In the yard he saw the remains of a bonfire with charred pieces of clothing, food tins and what appeared to be metal fittings from Army equipment; in the garden was a partly dug pit. The farm was thoroughly photographed and the exhibits officer added to the collection.

12

FOURTEEN THIEVES, A DRIVER & HIS MINDER

It's not possible to say who was first into the HVP when it stopped at Bridego Bridge, but Charlie Wilson was one of the first to smash his way in. The van was attacked from a side door, a window, and the rear door, which was a corridor-type door that would have led to the next carriage back – but that was back at Sears Crossing.

The first blow to the glass in the window of the door and the blow to the door at the rear were more or less simultaneous, and the terror this would have instilled to the men inside is beyond comprehension. They tried in vain to barricade themselves in but with five men being attacked on two or more fronts by twelve or more men, even though they were higher up in the carriage, it was not really a contest. The substitute driver and his minder had skulked back to one of the Land Rovers and at least one of the gang was minding Mr Mills and Mr Whitby on the grass embankment. It has been suggested that the phrase, 'They are barricading themselves in, get the guns!' was used to further terrify the Post Office staff but another historian has substituted another word for 'guns'. However, no firearms were used and the gang were soon in.

The Post Office staff were generally screamed and growled at and were soon overpowered, made to lie face-down and 'secured'. Bolt-cutters were brought in to cut a way into where the HVPs were. A chain of men from the carriage to the vehicles was formed and the robbery went ahead as 126 mailbags were removed, passed along the chain and down the embankment to the vehicles.

It was a smooth operation, almost military in its precision. Conversation was minimal and every man knew his role. Finally Mr Mills and Mr Whitby were forced up into the HVP carriage and with the five Post Office staff were told not to move for half an hour. The gang and their substitute train driver and his minder then disappeared into the night.

After about fifty minutes they arrived at the farm. There was some talk about a message on the radio – the gang had tuned into the police frequency – about 'someone nicking a train' but this is not confirmed though the time would be about right.

So £2.5 million, which weighed over two tons, was unloaded and dumped in the farm building. The vehicles were stored out of sight, and counting began. Roy James went to bed, and Gordon Goody went up to the first floor; he and Bob Welch listened to the police radio frequency. Buster Edwards started counting in what he later described as just a 'room full of paper'. At the million mark everyone viewed the pile. At some stage Tony Bennett was on the radio singing 'It's the Good Life'. But one has to question if it was.

The gang members were under strict instructions not to harm anyone, but they did, and I understand this was later discussed back at the farm. However, with the success of the raid the euphoria took over.

They were also told to keep their gloves on in the farm. It would be quite likely their names would be among the first to leap into police minds as the robbery was investigated, but without evidence they couldn't be arrested. And they left no evidence at all on either the signals, telephone wires, on the locomotive or the HVP carriage; they were all unidentifiable, apart from by the evidence they left at the farm.

It was August and the weather mild. It has been suggested that because they were there for a day longer – originally the raid was to take place the previous night but the word from their observers was that the load was light – so did the gloves shrink with sweat, or did prolonged wearing irritate the wearers? Either way, the following men left fingerprints or palm-prints at the farm: John Daly, Bruce Reynolds, Tommy Wisbey, Bob Welch, Jim Hussey, Roy James and the driver's minder, Ronald Biggs.

*

Bruce was woken when the final total was reached – Buster simply said it was two and a half million.

13

NOT THE GOOD LIFE

When Mr Mills and Mr Whitby attended the casualty department of the Royal Bucks Hospital at Aylesbury they were still handcuffed together, which made treatment of Mr Mills difficult. The stories of Mr Mills's injuries varied widely in the ensuing years: anywhere between eight and thirty stitches, take your pick.

Initially the fire brigade was called to free the men and they cut the joining link between the right and left handcuff, but also a police officer appeared with a set of keys which released the men. Mr Whitby left the hospital and arrived home in Crewe that night. Mr Mills was detained for a couple of days for observation, which was normal routine after a head injury. He was discharged from hospital on Saturday 10 August and travelled back to Crewe with his wife. Mr Mills could now try and recover from his injuries.

The press coverage was relentless. The story was splashed all over the newspapers and the television and radio brought updates whenever airtime allowed. The picture of Mr Mills with his head bandaged became almost as famous as others in the news that year, like those of Mr Profumo or President Kennedy. A lesser-known portrait was one of Mr Mills, with his head still in bandages, with his baby grandson; Mr Mills was to become the centre of controversy over the robbery and a brief resume of his injuries usually accompanied most news titbits and major headlines. This attention was to have its effect on him.

*

The original intention of the gang, if the provisions at the farm were anything to go by, was that they were to lay low there for several weeks. There was talk of an arrangement on the Sunday after the robbery for an associate to travel up to the farm with a vehicle large enough for transporting a substantial amount of the money – a horsebox. Jimmy White had been instrumental in making a secret compartment in the lorry at the farm to take money and it was he who had started to paint the lorry to change its appearance, according to some at any rate; others say it was Gordon – it was actually Gordon who arranged for one of the Land Rovers, which was blue, to be sprayed khaki green, but this was prior to the robbery.

But word had come over the radio of the vehicles the gang were thought to have used. And then the announcement that the police would be looking within a 30-mile radius of where the raid had taken place caused some consternation, and questions about hanging around on the farm until the Sunday began to be asked.

This suited Roger and he announced he was leaving first thing on the Friday morning and had a room arranged, which in the event he didn't occupy for a couple of nights. But he had a bicycle and he left the farm. He made some phone calls to Brian Field and another of Bruce's contacts and generally holed up in a room he had booked into in a hotel in Oxford. The next day he bought a car and a morning paper that headlined the furore. On his return to the farm he showed his fellow gang members the paper but also told them that he hadn't seen the police in the immediate area. He loaded some of one of the other gang member's money into the car as well as his own. He also gave Jimmy White a lift into Oxford. They bought another car and Jimmy took the one Roger had first acquired and Roger took the later one.

14

PAINT

At this point Roger hit a major snag, which I'll explain in a moment but he introduced an old friend of his into the plot, with disastrous consequences.

Most of the robbers had some kind of network of associates to do the odd bit of legitimate work, which ranged from the quite honest to shades the other way. Before a job like this the friends would all be briefed and ready for their task. One of Roger's associates was a bank manager who would launder the money for him and I gather this was done through a series of accounts. So Roger contacted him after he had left the farm in order that this part of the plan could go ahead. But much to his inconvenience and annoyance, when he contacted this associate, he seemed very agitated and said he wasn't able to help Roger. There was such a furore that everyone was talking about the money – it was all over the newspapers and there was a semi-permanent commentary on the radio and television.

Roger wasn't too bothered that the police were looking for the hideout because, although he knew his name would be in the frame as he was known to rob trains, he was sure he'd left no fingerprints or other traces on either the railway or at the farm. He was, however, bothered about his scuppered plan and so needed to think of an alternative quickly.

Roger went through a list of his friends and associates, mentally dismissing each as they came to mind. But one stood out as someone he could use. His name was Bill Boal and he lived with his wife and children and mother-in-law in Fulham.

Roger got in contact – there was talk of him turning up at the house, but this isn't clear. However, Roger got his man, and Bill arranged to travel to Oxford to meet him. The fact that Roger owed Bill several hundred pounds seems to have been a bait. But even though they'd known each other for many years, Bill wasn't a part of Roger's criminal world. It was said that Bill was in awe (if that's the right term) of Roger and wondered if one day his friend would include him in one of his crimes.

In the past Bill had a small excursion into crime; he had a conviction for being 'unlawfully on premises', and in the late 1940s he'd been to prison for handling stolen goods – a suit. Roger was on the periphery of this but the police didn't charge him. When Bill went inside the two men lost touch but after his release they met by chance at a dog racing meeting.

Bill had another conviction that I want to discuss a little later because the story is complicated, and it is best to approach this part of it chronologically.

*

William (Gerald) Boal was the youngest son of Thomas and Margaret and was born in Durham in 1914. He married Renee Richbell in Fulham, London in 1952 and they settled down there, where they had three children: two boys and a girl. Mrs Richbell, Renee's mum, lived with them too. Bill had his own business as a precision engineer and was a kind father, though it sounds as though Renee was 'the boss'.

He had a workshop in Queens Road in Mortlake not far from Barnes Hospital and is remembered even now by some of his work neighbours. I gather Bill's neighbours in Fulham always spoke well of him. He was eccentric and had some prejudices which didn't help him, but as a self-employed sole worker he managed to get along okay. He didn't like trades unions, so working for others would be a problem, and having people work for him may also have presented difficulties. But as his world was, it seemed well settled.

*

In Oxford, Roger was revising his plan. His 'whack' was in a collection of suitcases and he was also said to be carrying some money belonging to one of the other robbers. The money from the other robber is vague so unless he met Roger to collect it late on the Friday night then it seems to be missing.

Roger was sure the suitcases with his money in were safe in Oxford, so on the Saturday morning he drove with Bill to Bournemouth, where Bill had some old friends. When they got there, though, he couldn't find them at their old address. However, Roger was able to rent a flat easily enough and wondered if he could hide some of his money in Bournemouth. He continued to fine-tune his plan, and later dropped Bill off in Winchester to catch a train back to London.

Roger drove up to Oxford the following day to collect the money he had left and met Bill with his family at the station. The whole entourage then travelled to Bournemouth, where Renee was dropped off with their children to spend the afternoon on the beach. Meanwhile, Roger and Bill unloaded the money at the flat he'd rented.

He bought two cars in which he could hide the money and had formed a plan of renting garages to store them; having gained the use of one garage he saw an advert for another. When Mrs Clarke agreed to rent them a second garage things seemed to be working out.

Unfortunately Mrs Clarke was a policeman's widow quite unused to seeing men with large wads of cash wanting to pay her three months' rent in advance. She contacted the police. When Roger and Bill returned to park one of the cars in the garage, two of Bournemouth's CID officers were in close proximity. The policemen approached and a fracas ensued with Roger. Bill then pretended to be a passing citizen who went to help this poor middle-aged man against two (plain-clothed police) men. Both Roger and Bill were detained when another couple of police officers arrived in a car.

So after less than a week, life for Roger Cordrey turned towards one of Her Majesty's institutions courtesy of Detective Sergeant Stanley Davies and Detective Constable Charles Case of the Bournemouth Police, following information received from Mrs Emily Clarke.

At first Roger and Bill denied any knowledge of each other but that ruse would have been a bit transparent when it was discovered they both had a key to the same flat.

When they got to Police HQ in Bournemouth the two were searched and the property found in their possession logged individually on the charge sheets, and placed in separate bags. DS Davies was meticulous about this and this was later to his credit because when, at trial, counsel suggested the property of the two men was mixed, DS Davies could say the property was quite definitely kept separate.

Things didn't look good for Bill because he had the keys to one of the cars, an Austin A35. When the police found the keys they went in search of the car, and when they found it and opened the boot they found a suitcase which contained £56,047. Things got worse because it was Bill's handwriting on a label tied to another set of keys for another garage where a set of suitcases yielded a further £78,982. So then the police searched the flat Roger had rented and found yet more money – £5,910. It was said that both men admitted the money had come from the train, but they later denied this.

Meantime, officers from the Metropolitan Police went to Bill's home in Fulham and searched it; Mrs Renee Boal was arrested for receiving stolen money. Roger's sister and brother-in-law, May and Arthur Pilgrim, were also arrested on the same charge.

So Bill Boal was caught with Roger Cordrey and between them they had a total of £142,217 0*s* 0*d*.

DSupts Fewtrell and McArthur with DS Pritchard travelled to Bournemouth. Under caution the prisoners each made statements to DSupt Fewtrell and DS Pritchard to account for their activities since the day of the train robbery and explain how the money came to be in their possession. The evidence of the money in the suitcases left a lot to be explained. Both men were charged with conspiracy to rob and with robbery. They were also charged with three counts each of receiving stolen money.

After a long day at the seaside the three police officers finally left with two extra passengers; they arrived at Aylesbury at 9.30 p.m.

*

It does seem unfortunate that Bill was enticed into this web from which he couldn't escape but his position wasn't helped by his attitude – at least one officer from Bucks Police has described him thus: 'He was a mouthy sod.' And DS Davies said, 'Boal blew hot and cold ... He started screaming and became quite violent.'

In Bournemouth he was quoted to have said specifically about the money, 'Fair enough, it came from the train job.'

I discuss this type of evidence later, but briefly this was a statement Bill allegedly made that he later denied. At least one of the two police officers who arrested him attributed these words to Bill and it's likely their hearing of these words became a matter of evidence used against him, but this might be illegal. Evidence couldn't be used unless the person had been cautioned, but the argument might run that this was not evidence against him it was merely what a police officer heard him say, so it became part of the officers' evidence generally about the arrest. This was common in those days and it was called 'verballing'.

But why would the police want to attribute something to Bill he might not have said?

In the next part of this chapter I want to discuss another part of the evidence against Bill in which the police attempted to link him to the train robbery, the farm, and another of the robbers. Again it will be discussing the fabrication of evidence.

But why would the police want to attribute something to Bill he might not have done?

The verbal and other evidence saw him convicted of crimes he hadn't committed and he was to be sentenced to twenty-four years.

The crime he had committed, however, was to receive a few hundred pounds, and another man who received a comparable amount was sentenced to one year. Bill did handle stolen money and probably knew it was stolen. For this he might have faced a sentence of two to four years. Almost certainly the sentences for receiving and handling in this context would run concurrently and with remission Bill might have been out in about two years.

Bill denied being a part of the conspiracy or the robbery or ever being at the farm, and any evidence suggesting that he was is dubious to say the least. But why would the police target Bill, 'verbal' him and plant evidence on him? The answer might lie in the gap I left above in his criminal record (CRO No. 30624/47), which lists his most recent conviction on 19 April 1963 – 'Assault on Police'.

*

Bill was an engineer and was a man whose jacket pockets were full of odd bits and pieces. And with jackets, if one has metal objects in them that might not be 'regular', like a coin, then the fabric might tend to fray in places and small objects might fall through the pockets and into the lining.

There are two reports of small items found in Bill's jacket. One was said to have been found in a search of his home and another doesn't have details recorded. However, the report is that a small 'knob' of metal was found in the lining of his jacket and this small 'knob' was said to link Bill with the robbery because it linked him to Leatherslade Farm and linked him to another robber, Gordon Goody. The police said both men had been in contact with paint found at the farm.

*

The reason the police said this 'knob' was important was because it was stained with the yellow paint. This shows some remarkable powers of observation that a small 'knob' with a small 'fleck' of paint on it should become a focal point. But there was a tin of yellow paint at the farm and also someone had hand-painted the front of the Austin truck in yellow.

However, before I take things any further it was demonstrated at the Court of Appeal later that the paint evidence against Bill was considered inconclusive and the conviction for robbery was quashed, his sentence for conspiracy being reduced to fourteen years too. But the point in this part of the story is that evidence seems to have been manufactured, and this is why it is an important part of the history.

For years a great many people have said that the fingerprint evidence was not as reliable as it should have been, and in certain circumstances it might be possible to transfer a fingerprint from one surface to another; this is a bit far-fetched and not something I intend to pursue, but the paint evidence can be demonstrated to have been doubtful in its integrity. This doesn't mean I want to shy away from a discussion on the fingerprint evidence, but rather that I think the paint evidence demonstrates more wholly that evidence was questionable.

As an aside, all of the train gang said Bill Boal was not part of their plans or the robbery and he was not at Leatherslade Farm. DSupt Fewtrell even said publicly that he didn't think Bill was connected either with the major conspiracy or the robbery itself – and he would have been a party to the collecting of evidence. In fact it was he who quoted DS Davies from Bournemouth. But it's unclear in precisely what part of the enquiry his doubts started to creep in. DS Slipper said that eventually he doubted Bill was involved, but that doubt came over a number of years.

Mr Justice Edmund Davies said he was satisfied Bill was not one of the leading conspirators. Later Roger Cordrey said on oath that Bill was not a conspirator; DCS Butler also gave evidence at the same time (in a court case brought because the police and insurance companies wanted to seize the cars Roger and Bill had bought. But Bill's argument was that he legitimately owned one of the cars, so the matter had to go to court) but even with Roger and DCS Butler, all came to nothing.

The fleck of paint on the 'knob' found in Bill's pocket matched paint found at the farm – but Bill said he didn't own this 'knob' and hadn't seen it before. In some of the documentation this 'knob' is referred to as a watch-winder and if it was from a pocket watch might have been a half an inch or so in length; but if it was from the mechanism of a wristwatch, it would be tiny. One has to ask why this tiny piece of metal was subjected to such a thorough forensic examination. In order to draw attention to the paint, it would have had to be visible to the naked eye. I say this just to try and establish something about its size as I was unable to find any information on it.

The point was that Bill said he didn't own this watch-winder; this 'knob' on which there was a fleck of paint.

So there was paint found at the farm and paint found on a 'knob' in Bill's jacket.

In court Dr Holden swore the paints were so alike as to make the possibility of finding them in two separate places almost impossible. He said that if his life depended on it he wouldn't try and search for a similar paint as the odds against finding it were so high. But it would have been said in summing up that this didn't amount to proof that Bill had been to the farm. The fact that Dr Holden went to Bill's house and also examined a neighbour's house only served to tell him where the paint didn't come from which didn't help in court. Even though at appeal the evidence was said to be inconclusive, one wonders what the jury thought. In the event the charge of robbery was quashed at appeal but everyone had said Bill was innocent of robbery and conspiracy anyway.

But at this point a strange comparison of Bill's alleged behaviour can be made. According to the Bournemouth CID, Bill had said about the money in the suitcase, 'Fair enough, it came from the train job.' So one has to ask why he would move himself so close to a conviction for robbery but deny the ownership of a 'knob' that had paint on it and was in his pocket.

In the police report it was said that Bill's house was searched and in a jacket was found a 'knurled knob of yellow paint ... the same colour and chemical composition as that found on Goody's shoes'.

In the Court of Appeal judgement document the paint evidence is worded in a significantly different way: 'The paint-stained knob suggested that Boal had had an actual connection with Leatherslade Farm.'

A problem with any evidence is the way in which it can be presented. Counsel for the prosecution presented the paint evidence in a way that attempted to link Bill's 'knob' of paint with Gordon's shoes which, in turn, linked Gordon forensically with the farm through the paint. This could have been a bit of dramatic immediacy, as Bill and Gordon were both in the same dock in the same court; it was linking one with the other in the here-and-now sense rather than linking either separately with a farm some distance away.

There is another issue about the paint that should be discussed.

'Paint-stained'; paint is a liquid that, when applied to a surface, dries and protects and decorates. Stain means to mark or discolour or to change the colour of ... by applying a liquid substance.

I've never read anywhere of any fingerprint evidence on any 'knob' taken from Bill's jacket. Fingerprint evidence would confirm that Bill had contact with the item and therefore it wasn't evidence that lacked integrity. But if no fingerprint evidence was offered it suggests that Bill's link with the 'knob' – particularly as he denied seeing the item before – isn't demonstrated. It may be considered as over-dramatic to suggest that the 'knob' should have been subjected to fingerprint analysis, but according to the police the paint on it linked the 'knob' to the farm. And finding the 'knob' in his jacket linked the 'knob' to him. In fact, it doesn't – the rule of evidence would say it linked the paint on the 'knob' to Bill's jacket only – a fingerprint would link it to Bill. It was said to be inconclusive evidence.

If Dr Holden said the paint found on Bill and the paint found at the farm were virtually the same, then it still leaves the question of how the paint got onto the 'knob'. There are a number of ways, but what they come down to, and assuming Bill did own the 'knob', is that either the 'knob' came out of Bill's pocket or the paint went into it. The paint was on the 'knob' but there was no evidence that paint was present in any other form on the jacket, which more than suggests that the paint didn't leap up from the tin or floor or Gordon's shoes and attach itself to the 'knob' in his pocket. So as there were no other traces of paint in the pocket, the 'knob' doesn't seem to have been anywhere near Bill's pocket when the paint made contact with it.

So that leads to the suggestion that if paint had 'stained' the 'knob' it would be in liquid form when it had contact with the 'knob'. And as the paint was found at the farm, then the most likely scenario is that the 'knob' went to where the paint was and then went into Bill's pocket. If Bill wasn't at the farm but the 'knob' was, then the only suggestion left is some kind of interference by a third party. As there is no proof Bill was at the farm this seems probable and is supported by the lack of any evidence to link Bill with the 'knob', except to say it was in his pocket – but then the question emerges of how it got there.

So one arrives at the consideration that either the paint was taken to the 'knob', or the 'knob' was taken to the paint.

A pot of paint is portable, but one has to conclude that taking the pot of paint to Bill's jacket seems a bit far-fetched. Would it be possible then to take the 'knob' to the paint? The answer would seem to be that it would, and if one wanted to use discretion then this seems to be the obvious way. Then they could apply the paint to the 'knob' in its liquid form which, once dry, would explain the description of the 'knob' as 'paint-stained' and if it was dry before finding its way back into Bill's pocket it wouldn't leave any other trace of paint in the pocket. The paint stain might have been small, but even so, unless paint was applied to it away from the pocket, then it would have to be dry before it was returned to the pocket.

The only thing this third-party couldn't do was get Bill's fingerprints on the 'knob'. It's also unclear when the small 'knob' was stained with the paint; it may have been found at the farm already with paint on it.

But the only way this 'knob' could have got into Bill's pocket without any fingerprints on it would be if someone else put it there, which could be the reason that it was not 'forensically' linked to him through fingerprints. Evidence of fingerprints were offered from Monopoly pieces; I'm not sure why a watch-winder so essential to the prosecution should escape from this scrutiny.

So the evidence is not conclusive of Bill acting in a criminal way, save for the fact he was in possession of and handled stolen money, and the 'knob' might be a demonstration that evidence was tampered with or made up. Indeed, if there is anything to the suggestion that evidence against Bill was tampered with, then the suggestion that evidence against the others was tampered with becomes difficult to resist.

*

The paint evidence against Bill wasn't the only place where this type of evidence was said to appear. Some dubious evidence against Gordon was found on a pair of shoes. This matched paint found at the farm and also paint on the clutch pedal of one of the Land Rovers.

There was quite an alarming time lapse between the paint being found on his shoes, on the clutch pedal of the Land Rover and on the floor at the garage in the farm. This time lapse, though dubious, doesn't prove anything. Gordon was a thief who conspired and robbed the train as he now freely admits. But to this day denies the evidence of the paint is genuine.

Most of the robbers said they wanted to shout out at the court that Bill was neither involved in the conspiracy nor the robbery. But they couldn't because they all pleaded 'not guilty', so if they were saying they were neither at the track nor at the farm then they wouldn't know Bill wasn't there. After they'd been sentenced it was not possible either, because of the appeals they were to make.

Bill was allowed to leave prison about a week before the terminal illness he'd developed killed him, just about halfway through his sentence even though there was, by this time, parole. The problem with this and the reason Roger was paroled the following year is that Roger pleaded guilty, which he was, so was given parole; Bill pleaded not guilty, which he was, so didn't get parole. It has been said that parole is to let the guilty go free but keep the innocent or 'unrepentant' inside.

Nearly fifty years on there are still two issues that will affect the robbers in conversation. The name Jack Mills will prompt a strong response and a silence. The name Bill Boal will prompt a strong response and a strong description of how they felt he was dealt with.

It has long been held that the paint on the 'knob' was dubious evidence and if Bill swore he didn't own it, irrespective of the fact that it had paint on it that was said to come from the farm, one has to wonder how it got where it was found.

*

Another complication of the paint evidence was that there were two colours of paint involved: yellow and khaki. The khaki paint had previously been sprayed on the stolen Land Rover as it had originally been blue.

The yellow paint was applied to the lorry the robbers used, probably as a way of disguising its identity, and because the impression of the three vehicles was that of an Army convoy it seems absurd to think the lorry was painted before the raid. However, it was said that paint from Gordon's shoe was on the clutch pedal of one of the Land Rovers. If the yellow paint on the lorry was applied after the raid and the Land Rovers were parked away from the lorry so that they couldn't be seen from the air, it's doubtful they were moved after the raid. The crime-scene photographs show quite clearly that they were concealed when the farm had been deserted. So why would Gordon later get into the Land Rover so neatly concealed? And the Land Rover was found across the yard in another shed. As to his not leaving paint on the floor of the Land Rover in front of the driver's seat, this is equally as puzzling.

The theory was this. Gordon got into the Land Rover, and as he got into it he placed his left foot on the clutch and nowhere else. To get into a vehicle the body makes a complex movement, transferring the weight from both feet to one foot and then to one's posterior. If the body is in the process of transferring its position by getting into a vehicle then usually the hands are holding onto something, like the door or steering wheel to aid balance – then one moves sideways into the vehicle, hip first. But logic dictates that the left leg would be utilised as part of the balancing mechanism and so would go onto the floor of the vehicle first, not the clutch. Some drivers get into their vehicle and, once sat behind the steering wheel, they adjust their body position to ensure the best position in which to drive with comfort and efficiency, the best position to engage with the foot pedals. They might adjust the seat, the mirror or other things, but it is the positioning of the body that attracts my attention. In short, I ask, how does one get into a vehicle with a fairly large blob of paint on the soles of one's shoe, settle the body to drive comfortably, and then proceed to drive but the only trace of paint from the sole of the shoe is on the clutch pedal?

*

It is so difficult to escape the description of the two lots of paint evidence without asking just how the paint got on the 'knob' in Bill's pocket and nowhere else in the pocket; and how the paint from Gordon's shoes got on the clutch pedal of the Land Rover and nowhere else in the Land Rover. And it also seems that the paint wasn't touched until after the raid, when Gordon didn't seem to have any reason to go near the Land Rover.

15

AND THE REST LEFT

Bruce and John rose early on the Friday morning and were soon on their way.

Roger had returned late that morning and loaded a Wolseley car he'd bought. He also loaded some of Frank's money and left the farm with Jimmy White. Roger had some accommodation arranged in Oxford so unloaded the money into a Rover he'd bought there. Jimmy then took the car and returned to the farm. The Wolseley was then passed over to Alf Thomas, who loaded up and left.

Bruce and John returned later that evening with an accomplice and two Austin Healey cars. Jimmy White departed with one of these cars. John and Stan (their train driver) with the accomplice left in the accomplice's car. Bruce and Ronnie Biggs departed in the second Austin Healey.

Roy had previously left for London and by the time he returned to the farm it was late on the Saturday night. The place was deserted and it did occur to him the police might have moved in and they were now waiting to pounce on him, so all he could do was return to London and await a call from the others.

The remaining eight robbers had left for Karin and Brian Field's house on the Saturday evening. They had driven up to the farm; Karin in the family Jaguar and Brian in a van, and an accomplice drove a second van. Brian had only intended to deliver the two vans they'd got for the gang, and then depart. A couple of the robbers said they were going back to the Fields' house with them. Brian had never intended to get this close to the robbery but as the robbers had been compelled to change their plans now that the police had made their search a public piece of news, they looked to him to help. He didn't really have much choice, but when the remaining of the eight also said they were coming he nearly needed hospital attention. However, Karin was a bit more receptive to this.

By the evening of Saturday the farm was deserted and all ready for the cleaner to come in to remove all of the evidence and fingerprints; this was the man Brian first introduced to Gordon and Buster and he had accompanied the Ulsterman. But the cleaner didn't come in to remove all the evidence and fingerprints.

16

THE GENERAL INVESTIGATION

Comdr Hatherill and DCS Millen had travelled up to Bucks Police HQ to discuss matters with DSupts McArthur and Fewtrell on 13 August, and here they could also visit Leatherslade Farm. DSupt McArthur had recently been promoted and was now affiliated to the Murder Squad rather than the Flying Squad. So to replace him as lead of the actual investigation was a detective with a keen eye for the London underworld: Detective Chief Superintendent Thomas Butler, who was a member of the Flying Squad. The team was expanding but it meant that DCS Butler, assisted by Detective Chief Inspector Peter Vibart, could look after the robbery and search for the robbers while DSupt McArthur could turn his attention to the preparation of evidence to be presented to the DPP's office when the time came.

DCS Butler was a London lad and had grown up in Fulham. He had a married sister and their brother had been killed in action in 1943. Tommy lived with his mother and was reputed to work up to eighteen hours a day. His driving was terrible and his subordinates would do almost anything to avoid his passenger seat! He was known by some as one of the finest detectives of his era and carried the name 'the Silver Fox'. When paired with DCI Vibart they were known as 'the Terrible Twins'.

*

Only a few households in the 1960s were two-car families and Mr John Ahern and his wife were no exception: Mrs Ahern was a housewife and didn't have a job. But she took in the odd bit of sewing, which helped out the family budget and allowed them Continental holidays. The second vehicle in the family was an old, eccentric motorcycle that cut out when it overheated, but as his car was in for service on 16 August, Mr Ahern was to travel into work on this. He would give his friend and colleague Mrs Esa Hargreaves a lift.

When the motorcycle overheated and cut out they were near Redlands Woods, which bordered Dorking in Surrey. While the motorcycle recovered, Mr Ahern and Mrs Hargreaves wandered into the woods, or at any rate that's the story they gave. Here they were surprised to find a camel leather briefcase, a brown leather briefcase, a holdall and, a little further into the woods, a brown leather suitcase; certainly not the sort of things one would expect to find. With no other people in the vicinity, they investigated further and found the bags contained rather a lot of money. They stopped another motorist and asked him to call the police.

At about 9.00 a.m. Detective Inspector Basil West, of the Surrey Police, arrived and took possession of the cases. The money was later counted and totalled £100,900.

Detective Constable Alexander Illing, of the Surrey Police, examined the cases for fingerprints and as he did so he found in the camel leather briefcase an account from a German hotel for the previous February, made out for a Herr and Frau Field. This account was in a narrow pocket in the lining. On the brown leather briefcase he found a number of fingerprints. These fingerprints were photographed in their entirety. The photographs taken were referred to DSupt Ray for his examination, and the prints were identified as Brian Field's. Brian and his wife had stayed at the hotel the bill was made out for during the appropriate period.

According to the official police report, money was found in the camel leather briefcase and the brown suitcase, but the only report of fingerprints was on the brown leather briefcase. This might seem a departure into the minutiae of it all but when the police went to Brian's house with a search warrant a week or so later, he was quite calm and rational, certainly showing no outward appearances of a man likely to be arrested. The whole episode baffles.

So £100,900 in bags, some of the other bags in the drop bearing his fingerprints – but not the actual bags with money – and no report of any other fingerprints either identifiable or not. Is it a fact that Brian had a full 'whack', as the other men had, of £150,000? The robbers later said he did, and he does seem to still loom large in the overall story. And it was his contact who was to clean up the farm. On balance, then, with his role before the robbery and then again after and his involvement in the aftermath at the farm, and his help to get the robbers away from Leatherslade Farm, it would be fair to think he got a full £150,000 'whack'.

His house was searched but there was no sign of any incriminating evidence, so what happened to that other £49,100?

Then the question emerges of whether the bags were dumped by someone terrified and about to be arrested. Brian's behaviour a week or so later didn't suggest this. So the second question is, were they dumped or were they placed there? It seems little was done to conceal the bags.

So if the bags were placed there, then why? For someone to collect later doesn't seem to fit, and Brian would know that fingerprints would be traceable so the whole sense of it doesn't tally.

It might be that he'd left the money with a minder and the minder panicked and just dumped the money.

As far as I know, Brian never admitted he placed or dumped the bags in the wood, so it might be pure conjecture to follow this line. And if one thinks just for a second that he might have been far brighter than he was ever credited for, then it becomes clear that if he kept quiet and his role and the roles of the other Mr Field and Mr Wheater got bogged down with confusion, then he might be able to scrape out of it without a conviction for robbery – which he did – and without a conviction for conspiracy – which he did on appeal. The Court of Appeal took the line that even though there was a link between Brian and the cases, with the receipt and with fingerprints on the bags, that still didn't prove that it was he who received the money, nor that it was through him that the money arrived in the wood.

Brian would know that if he was going to use the case for the money then nothing traceable should be in it, or anywhere near it. The hotel bill doesn't sound as though it was concealed; it was just in the zipped side compartment. It doesn't make sense that he overlooked this. The same applies to the fingerprints. One is left with no alternative other than to at least acknowledge the question of who else might have had access to the bags.

The police got him because their web was a thorough one. He had denied knowing Lennie Field, despite evidence to the contrary; with his link to Mr Wheater he was unable to duck out of the conspiracy to obstruct justice, for which he got five years.

He left prison in 1967, by which time he was divorced, changed his name and disappeared.

We never did learn what became of the £49,100. Piers Paul Read attempted to make some kind of breakdown of the total figure and what had happened to it, and this left the books balanced when the various payments had been made and the 'whacks' had been distributed. Although this depended on what the robbers told him, there is no reason to believe Brian received anything less than a £150,000 full 'whack'. But the trail went cold, and never warmed up again.

As part of their investigation the police obtained a list of all phone numbers Brian's home phone connected to. Eight were public telephone boxes, but this didn't take the investigation anywhere.

When he was in prison Karin divorced him. This was all done quickly because she was pregnant with the child of a German journalist and if Karin was pregnant while still married to another man who was not a German, then it could affect the child's German citizenship. A degree absolute was given in court about two weeks before the due date. I couldn't find any record either in the UK or Germany of the birth or Karin's remarriage, if indeed she remarried.

Brian became Brian Carlton when he left prison. He married Sian and they lived in 'Carlton House' in the Richmond area. I couldn't find out anything about Brian's life there. I traced the sister of his third wife, Sian, but was unable to discover anything. I wanted to know what he was doing with his life, but in 1979 he and his wife were killed in a car crash; the driver of the other vehicle was above the legal alcohol limit.

The secret of the £49,100 must have died with him, but he was driving a Porsche!

*

About a week after the robbery, a sales assistant in a ladies' dress shop in Reigate became suspicious of a woman customer who bought a quantity of clothing and paid in dirty £1 notes. The woman behaved in such an unusual way that the shop assistant followed her out of the shop and saw her get into a car. She took the registration number, and described it as a small grey sports car, registration number REN 22. When she got back to the shop she phoned the police. Police Constables Donald Cooper and Gerald Bixley of Reigate located the car, and kept a close eye on it. Later they saw a man get in it and he gave his name as James Edward Patten. He was with the woman who had been into the dress shop. After a short discussion the policemen were satisfied there was nothing untoward and drove away.

But there was something about the couple which prompted the policemen to make a few enquiries, and it transpired that the couple had been to a number of shops. At one shop Mr Patten had given his name as Mr Ballard: Clovelly Caravan Site, Boxhill, Surrey.

So the police paid the site a visit and it was discovered that a Mr Bollard had bought a caravan there. The caravan was searched and £136 in £1 notes was found in a jacket pocket.

Police kept watch on the caravan and on 18 August one Harry John Brown was stopped entering it. He was interviewed but there was insufficient evidence to arrest him. However, enquiries were in hand and Mr Ballard and Mr Patten were identified as

Jimmy White. A search of the panelling in the caravan revealed £30,440. Some of the notes were identified as being part of the money stolen in the robbery. It was all handed over to DSupt Fewtrell on 20 August.

The caravan was examined for fingerprints and there were a number of articles on which fingerprints were found; these were identified as those of Jimmy White and Lily Mercy Price, alias Sheree White, his wife. DC Illing also found fingerprints on a milk bottle, and all items were sent to DSupt Ray's department for comparison. They belonged to Jimmy and Sherree White.

On 21 August, the caravan was taken to Bucks Police HQ at Aylesbury.

More enquiries were made about Mr Patten/Bollard/White. The address he gave the two policemen at Reigate was looked into, and it seemed that Mr and Mrs Patten took the tenancy of a flat in Beulah Hill, South London on 25 March 1962, at £295 per annum and paid their rent quarterly in advance. No payment had been made since the last quarterly payment commencing on 24 June 1963. Mrs Patten was last seen at the flat on 27 July. On Monday 29 July, Mr Patten telephoned the daily woman and said that his wife had gone on holiday.

The Austin Healey car, REN 22, was purchased on 9 August for £900 at a garage in the Kings Road by a man giving the name of Mr John Steward, of Chaunston Road, Taunton, Somerset, which of course was false. The £900 was made up mainly of £5 notes. On 10 August, an application was received by the London County Council for a twelve-month road fund licence from James Edward Patton of The Woodlands, Beulah Hill.

What is a bit of a puzzle is that it was supposedly Bruce and John and their accomplice who arrived at the farm on 9 August with two Austin Healey cars. Possibly, though, if they'd only bought the cars that day then the documents wouldn't have been sent off for registration and change of ownership. Jimmy could do this later.

About a week after the robbery the Austin Healey was left at a garage for repair and Jimmy didn't collect it. On 21 August, the car was taken to Chalk Farm Police Garage.

*

Going back to the gang's vehicles, they were:

A new Land Rover, which had the registration BMG 757A, which was false. It was originally light blue but had been painted a khaki colour. It had been stolen from Oxenden Street, in London, on 21 July.

The Land Rover with the genuine registration number of BMG 757A was ex-War Department and was part of an auction of ex-War Department vehicles at Ruddington, Nottinghamshire, where it was sold on 2 July 1963 to a London motor dealer. It was then re-sprayed Deep Bronze Green. The dealers, Cross Country Vehicles, resold their vehicles to the public through Exchange and Mart. On 26 July they received a phone call from a Mr Bentley about the Land Rover and later two men called to see it. One of them agreed to buy the Land Rover for £195; he returned to collect it with the registration number plate on either 3 or 4 August. Mr Bentley was later identified as Jimmy White.

The lorry was an Austin Goods Platform Truck, BPA 260. When the police found it at Leatherslade Farm it was dark green in colour with the front and cab painted yellow. It was traced as having passed through the auction of ex-War Department vehicles on 24 April, when it had been purchased by D. A. Mullard & Company Limited, of Edgware. They re-sprayed it olive green. It was then bought by a Mr F. Blake of Kenton Lane, Middlesex, for £300. On 30 July Mr Blake collected the vehicle, saying he had registered it. He didn't have the number plates with him and chalked a registration number on the original blanks. Mr Blake was Jimmy White.

The number BPA 260 was actually registered to a Ford motorcar that had been broken up by a scrap dealer in Gloucester a few years earlier.

The lorry was found to have a road fund licence that had been stolen in London a few weeks before the robbery. The police at Bethnal Green had recorded the theft.

17

MORE ARRESTS

As I discussed earlier, following the arrests of Roger and Bill in Bournemouth, the Metropolitan Police made three more arrests. Roger's sister and her husband, May and Arthur Pilgrim, were taken in for receiving just over £1,700, and Bill's wife Renee had allegedly received £1,190.

On 22 August, Charlie Wilson was arrested by Flying Squad officers at his home in Clapham in South London and charged with being concerned in the robbery. Charlie denied having been either to Cheddington or Leatherslade Farm, but his fingerprints and palm-prints were found at Leatherslade Farm, on a windowsill in the kitchen, on a Saxa salt drum and on a cellophane wrapping of a Johnson's traveller kit found in the kitchen.

On 24 August Robert William Pelham, a twenty-six-year-old motor fitter of Notting Hill, London, was arrested and charged with receiving £545. He had been a mechanic who admired the skill of Roy James, and had worked with him and known him for a while. In court his counsel argued the £551 Mr Pelham took from Roy was payment for a new engine. He was acquitted.

Also on the evening of 24 August, Surrey CID officers from Reigate went to Ronnie Biggs's house. His wife, Charmian, had been spending a lot of money but Ronnie said he'd won £510 on horse racing, which DI Morris was able to verify. Ronnie was asked if he knew any of the men wanted in connection with the train robbery and he said, 'I knew Reynolds some years ago. I met him when we were doing time together in Wandsworth.'

Ten days later the Flying Squad was back to arrest Ronnie and they took him to New Scotland Yard, where DCS Butler was waiting to interview him. Anything he said was taken down, but he refused to sign the document; he was told he would be taken to the Bucks Police HQ at Aylesbury, where he would be charged. He was then formally cautioned. Fingerprints found on a Monopoly box, a Pyrex plate and a bottle of ketchup at the farm were his. He claimed that he was at home on 7/8 August 1963, and remembered 8 August in particular because it was his birthday. He denied ever visiting Leatherslade Farm.

On 7 September Flying Squad officers went to Dog Kennel Hill, London, to see Jim Hussey. They had a search warrant, but nothing was found to connect him with the robbery. He was taken to New Scotland Yard where he was seen by DCS Butler, and he denied having anything to do with the robbery or having visited Leatherslade Farm, Brill or Oakley. He also denied knowing any of the other people charged, or anyone who had been circulated by the press as being wanted for the robbery. He was questioned about the Land Rover and the lorry used in the robbery, but denied any knowledge of them. A statement was taken from him under caution to confirm this.

Jim Hussey was taken to Bucks Police HQ in Aylesbury, where he was charged with committing robbery. His fingerprints and palm-prints were taken and later compared by DSupt Ray with marks he found at the farm, and a palm-print matched one found on the tailboard of a lorry.

When the home of Bob Welch, who was arrested on 25 October, was searched, a hotel bill was found in the name of Richards showing that five men stayed at the Flying Horse Hotel, Nottingham, on 22 May. When this bill was examined for fingerprints by DSupt Ray, a print was found that belonged to Jim Hussey. Subsequently the hotel receptionist picked Jim out at an identification parade at Aylesbury as being one of the five men who stayed there. She couldn't say whether he was Mr Richards and was unable to make any other identification. It was a Mr Richards who had made enquiries at Midland Marts about the farm.

On 11 September, Tommy Wisbey was taken to New Scotland Yard by Flying Squad officers. He was first seen on 20 August, when he visited New Scotland Yard. He explained his movements on 7 and 8 August 1963, which were taken down in a statement which he signed. On 11 September he telephoned New Scotland Yard and was seen by two Flying Squad officers and later by DCS Butler. He denied knowing Brill, Oakley, Leatherslade Farm, or any of the people who'd been charged with the robbery. He made a statement under caution confirming his original one. Mr Wisbey was then told he was to be charged with the robbery and cautioned. He was taken to Aylesbury and charged. His fingerprints and palm-prints were taken and forwarded to DSupt Ray, where they were compared with prints found at Leatherslade Farm. They were identical to those found on an attachment to the bath at the farm.

On 14 September, Lennie Field, a merchant seaman of Harringay, was arrested for the robbery. He was identified as the man who was or had been in the process of buying Leatherslade Farm. The solicitor designated Mr Field on the contract. A deposit of £555 was paid on the price of £5,550 on 23 July, with possession on exchange of contracts, but before completion. Possession was requested and arranged for 29 July. The solicitor signed his half of the contract on behalf of his client, which was unusual.

On 15 September, Brian Field was arrested for the robbery. On 16 August a number of bags containing £100,900 had been found in strange circumstances, as discussed. The fingerprints on the case and the hotel bill were cited.

During the enquiries into the sale of Leatherslade Farm, the association between Lennie Field and Brian Field was established, but they were not related.

*

Other residents of Bridle Road in Whitchurch where Brian Field lived told the police that a great many vehicles came to his house on Friday evening, 9 August, and the traffic continued for most of the weekend. In fact some of the neighbours said they were unable to sleep because of the number of cars and vans. This was said to continue until the Sunday morning, but there was some doubt as to the accuracy of this.

*

The police's view was that anyone who was involved in buying Leatherslade Farm or had made that intention known would be considered as an accessory to the robbery, and anyone who assisted in the acquisition of the farm would be a party to the conspiracy to rob.

Brian Field had gone to the farm with Lennie Field.

The police expected that anyone who had heard of the farm and knew about it, and had recently been in some negotiation for its purchase, could assist the police by contacting them – if their intentions were honourable. But when Brian became aware that the farm had been found and, moreover, it was established that it had been the hideout of the robbers, he made no effort to report his knowledge to the police.

*

The Fraud Squad had been looking into the activities of the law team and that of the solicitor, John Wheater. He was arrested by Fraud and Flying Squad officers on 17 October.

There were two initial charges, and as with most of the others who appeared to be on the periphery of the activity, the first charge was of conspiracy to stop the mail train with intent to rob.

But it was the other charge which seemed the most certain to seal his undoing: that he, 'well knowing that one Leonard Denis Field had robbed Frank Dewhurst of 120 mailbags, did comfort, harbour, assist and maintain him'.

*

On 3 October, Gordon Goody was charged with conspiracy to stop a mail train with intent to rob, and with robbery. The evidence against him was, as described, complicated and was always considered controversial.

On 16 August, DSupt McArthur telephoned New Scotland Yard asking for Goody's home to be searched. This search was carried out by Flying Squad officers but nothing incriminating was found. Gordon wasn't present at the time of the search, but his mother, Mrs Evelyn Goody, was. She told the officers that Gordon had left for a short break a few days before, and that as far as she knew he was either at Ramsgate or Margate.

Mr Charles Alexander, who was the landlord of the Windmill pub in Blackfriars and was a good friend of Gordon, had lent him a car, a Sunbeam Rapier, on 22 August. Mr Alexander said later that Gordon had been a good friend of his for about ten years. With the car he was to drive up to Leicester to meet a Miss Margaret Perkins, and he'd booked a room at the Grand Hotel. On the journey up, the car broke down and had to be towed to a garage. He told the recovery mechanic his name was Charles Alexander, giving the Windmill pub as his address. Gordon completed the journey by taxi.

At the hotel, for reasons unclear, the staff were suspicious and called the police; one report said the staff thought he was Bruce Reynolds. Two CID officers turned up and Gordon gave them too the name of Mr Alexander. However, they discovered this was false and when they took him to the police station he admitted who he was and Bucks Police HQ were contacted.

DCI Vibart and Detective Sergeant Leonard Read travelled up to Leicester and they were keen to know his whereabouts at 3.00 a.m. on 8 August, but no matter how they put the question he avoided giving a straight answer.

He explained he'd been living at the Windmill pub since his mother's house had been searched. He said, 'Look I was away out of it, over the water on the Green Isle, so you can't fit me in.'

Back at Bucks Police HQ he was interviewed again, this time by DCS Butler and DCI Vibart. They followed up with another interview a couple of days later in which Gordon denied any knowledge of the farm. Later that night, DCS Butler and DCI Vibart followed the line of enquiry about his trip to Ireland and discovered he had actually returned to London on 6 August. When they confronted him with this he declined to make any further comment. But proving he was in the country at 3.00 a.m. on 8 August was one thing; proving he was at Sears Crossing, Bridego Bridge and Leatherslade Farm was quite another.

So they couldn't hold him and he was released at 12.15 a.m. on 25 August. But he was kept under close surveillance.

Miss Perkins had first met Gordon in London in June 1963, when she was living in Putney. Gordon had told her back in mid-July that he would be away on holiday in Ireland with his mother in August, but he would send her postcards each day he was there. Miss Perkins had arranged for him to send the postcards to her friend's home rather than hers, and the friend would pass them on to her. Her friend dutifully said she had received the postcards on 5, 6 and 7 August. Unfortunately the postcards were disposed of by Miss Perkins soon after, but it's doubtful that they would have given Gordon a good alibi anyway. The police knew he was back in England and that his alibi had been destroyed elsewhere down its chain, but this still wasn't enough for an arrest.

They had to either link him with the train or with the farm, and they knew his history of attacking evidence.

Flying Squad officers, together with Dr Holden, went to the Windmill pub in Blackfriars where Gordon said he stayed. They searched a room and found a pair of suede shoes which Mr Alexander could confirm were Gordon's.

According to the police report, 'Leatherslade Farm was examined and samples taken, a squashed tin of yellow paint was noticed in a shed where the Austin lorry had been kept. Following an examination of Mr Goody's shoes by Dr Holden and the finding of yellow paint on them this tin became significant.'

It was 23 August when Gordon was first taken into custody. Subsequent to this, a sample of paint on the Land Rover was taken to New Scotland Yard. The problem with this evidence is the possibility it was contaminated – the vehicles were taken from Leatherslade Farm on 19 August and they were driven away. On 28 August 1963 this tin was collected from the farm.

But it all comes back to the suggestion that the paint on Gordon's shoes was only found on laboratory examination. So why did the police take them?

For the police to take the shoes into custody, there must have been something visible on the shoes, or something about them when they found them in the Windmill pub. And if it was paint that was visible then Gordon would have got rid of them. He was that careful; one nickname he had was 'Checker'. If nothing was visible on the shoes then why did the police take them?

But it took nearly two weeks for paint to be collected from the farm, and then to be compared with that on Gordon's shoes. Two weeks for what was vital forensic evidence to be matched. The paint found on the clutch pedal of one of the Land Rovers suggested Gordon had been at the farm and also that he had driven the Land Rover. This seemingly tardy attitude to the evidence doesn't seem to get any better because the vehicles were further examined by Dr Holden on 6 September and again on 19 September. On 28 September, Dr Holden visited Leatherslade Farm with DCS Butler when further samples of yellow paint were taken from the garage floor.

Dr Holden's report said that the paint found on Gordon's shoes was identical in colour and chemical composition to samples of paint on the tin from Leatherslade Farm and the vehicles found there.

If Gordon had stepped into paint and then got into the Land Rover and had driven it then one would expect to see some of the paint on the carpet under the pedal, or would there have been some evidence of paint on the floor in front of the driver's seat deposited as he got into the vehicle? As discussed earlier, paint was not found in either part of the driver's seat well.

But Dr Holden was satisfied that Gordon's shoes had been at Leatherslade Farm. Following the trial, Dr Holden won damages for libel from a newspaper who claimed he had interfered with the evidence. Dr Holden seemed genuine with his evidence, but somewhere or other Gordon's shoes and the evidence found on Bill Boal had come into contact with paint which had been found at Leatherslade Farm. This proves Gordon's shoes and

Bill's small metal 'knob' had contact with paint; it doesn't prove either man was at Leatherslade Farm.

When arrested on 3 October, Gordon was seen by DCS Butler and DCI Vibart. He was accompanied by his solicitor, and he admitted the shoes were his and that he had never lent them to anyone. On the instructions of his solicitor he refused to answer any more questions. The evidence against Gordon was circumstantial and forensic, which would have been far superior to any eye-witness evidence, assuming it was true.

His defence was centred around the inconsistencies of where the paint might also have been expected to be in the vehicle's driver's seat well, but to no avail.

Years later he said in an interview that he was one of the robbers, that he had been on the train and at the farm. But the evidence against him had been fabricated. This means in collecting this evidence the law had been broken and a conspiracy had occurred. Evidence has to be collected lawfully and the penalties are severe. At the least Mr Justice Edmund Davies would have ruled the evidence inadmissible because otherwise the court would have been a party to the wrongdoing. The police had reason to hold a grudge against Gordon because he had made them look so foolish (probably not deliberately) at his trial for the wages snatch at Heathrow Airport the previous year. If a policeman suspects a villain to have done something he has to prove it; then the prosecution has to prove it. Then the conviction is proper.

There are folk who would condone the fabrication of evidence and say that the villain gets his just deserts. But that denies a fundamental right, and that is to a fair trial; Gordon ate his porridge for over twelve years. Fabricating evidence is lying to the state, the monarch and the people; if they do it against one and there is no objection, then they could do it to another – a completely innocent person, like Bill Boal. This is known as 'noble cause' corruption, where the police act as counsel, judge and jury. Is this the beginning of a police state or the sign of its maturity? It is now widely accepted that the paint from Leatherslade Farm was also planted on Bill Boal and he finished up with a fourteen-year sentence after appeal – the most he should have got for what he'd done, receiving or handling, would have been about two to four years imprisonment. So on our behalf Bill Boal was convicted of something he didn't do, and his family were left almost destitute – a decent, hard-working family. Jack Mills's family have ever since had people bleating for them and how badly Mr Mills was treated – they have a point, but Jack Mills and his family got seven more years. Bill Boal's family got nothing except a stigma – Bill Boal died in prison, or in a nursing home a week after his release. One of the last things he was quoted to have said was to protest his innocence.

I will return to Bill Boal later, and there is more to discuss about how the police attempted to collect evidence illegally.

*

Bobby Welch, a club proprietor of Islington, London, was arrested on 25 October by Flying Squad officers. The following day he was charged at Bucks Police HQ with conspiracy to stop the mail train with intent to rob it, and with robbery.

His house was searched on 14 August at the request of DSupt McArthur and a number of items were taken away for examination. Bob was out at the time of the search, though his wife was at home.

On 16 August he was seen by Flying Squad officers and questioned about his movements on 7 and 8 August. Bob made a written statement in which he said he'd never been to Aylesbury or, indeed, to that area. He later said in relation to the robbery, 'Do you mean the train job? I don't know anything about that, I don't even know Cheddington.'

During an interview with DCS Butler, Bob again denied knowing Leatherslade Farm, or the area surrounding it, or that part of the country. He also denied knowing any of the prisoners arrested at that time except Tommy Wisbey and Jim Hussey.

Bob's fingerprints and palm-prints were taken and compared with marks found at Leatherslade Farm. The palm-print was identical to marks on a Pipkin beer can left in a cupboard in the kitchen of Leatherslade Farm.

He was charged with robbery and conspiracy.

The Pipkin can was one of nine found at the farm. Some were empty, some full; this can was half full. It was found by DSupt Ray in the kitchen at the farm with two other full cans, and each was stamped '723'. Of the other cans, four had the same marking, but two cans were found on the bonfire and no marking could be seen. The beer, which was filled into the cans at the brewery of Friary Meux Limited at Guildford on 23 July, apparently had a short shelf life and wholesalers and retailers dealt with stocks in date order.

Bicester in Oxfordshire had become a focal point in the enquiries and is about 9 miles from Leatherslade Farm. On 7 August, ten cans of Pipkin were bought at an off-licence and the manager had records that he had received his supplies from the Ind Coope depot at Oxford on 1 August, which had received its supplies from Friary Meux Limited at Guildford. Pipkin cans from 30 July had the number '723' stamped on them. This batch was exhausted by 7 August. The finding of nine cans at Leatherslade Farm, seven of which bore the same number as those sold at Bicester, was considered proof that they were the same cans. In court, this evidence wasn't challenged.

But it was far from adequate to convict Bob, and one defence he could have put forward was that he handled the cans elsewhere quite innocently. Friary Meux Brewery was visited by DSupt McArthur and DS Pritchard, and the 2,500-odd cans of Pipkin in the batch bearing the mark '723' were investigated. A questionnaire was drawn up and, with a covering report, was sent to police stations. Officers were to visit retailers and ask them to complete the questionnaire, and any retailers that had sold six or more cans at any one time were to be questioned closely about the customer. This was followed up by the customer being traced and interviewed. The officers completed this part of the investigation and the prosecution felt confident that they could challenge any claim Bob made that he innocently handled the can. In the event, he put forward the argument of an innocent call at the farm after the robbery when he was offered beer from a Pipkin can.

A hotel bill had been found at Bob's home chargeable to a Mr Richards from the Flying Horse hotel, Poultry, Nottingham. This was for accommodation for five men on 22 May. It was a Mr Richards who visited Midland Marts Limited in Bicester on 24 June 1963 regarding the purchase of the farm. Bicester is where the Pipkin cans were bought.

Jim Hussey, who was in custody by this time, was the only fingerprint on Mr Richards's bill – but it was found in Bob Welch's sideboard.

So some of the evidence was far from conclusive and there was no proof that the Mr Richards who'd stayed at the hotel was the same man who visited Midland Marts Ltd.

*

On 2 December 1963, all prisoners arrested went before Linslade Magistrates. With the exception of Mrs Mary Manson, all were committed for trial for conspiracy to rob, robbery or receiving.

*

On 3 December, John Daly was arrested at an Eaton Square flat and charged with robbery.

At the farm a number of Monopoly tokens were found and examined by DSupt Ray. John's fingerprints were found on one of these tokens and on a piece of green cardboard.

The hunt, with the help of a media campaign, was started in late August, but after several weeks Scotland Yard announced John was a 'fugitive from justice'.

John Daly was well known to the police and had been seen on a few occasions, the last of which was just before 21 June 1963, but it's unclear what the police were following up at that point. He was then clean-shaven and weighed between 16 and 17 stone. On 3 December when he was arrested, he'd initially denied his identity, and gave the name Mr Grant. He was much thinner, weighing about 12 stone, and had grown a beard. He later admitted his identity but denied he'd ever been to Leatherslade Farm. He was charged.

In his book, Jack Slipper, who was then a detective sergeant, said that even Detective Chief Inspector Frank Williams was unsure at first if the man was actually John Daly.

*

On 10 December, Roy James, sometime silversmith and racing driver, was arrested by Flying Squad officers at a St John's Wood flat and charged with robbery.

At Leatherslade Farm, DSupt Ray examined a blue-edged glass plate and a Johnson's traveller's kit. On the plate and on the cellophane wrapping of the traveller's kit were some fingerprints which were identified as Roy's.

On 14 August, thirty-five mailbags were taken from Leatherslade Farm to Bucks Police HQ, emptied and the contents examined. The mass of papers and paper scraps were sorted and put into bags that were taken to New Scotland Yard for examination by DSupt Ray. On a loose page in a magazine were Roy James's fingerprints.

Following Roy's identification the media were again asked for help in tracing him. In August 1963 he was living in Chelsea, but he had a garage for his racing car in Battersea. Flying Squad officers went to his garage first and then to his flat. The flat was searched and although they didn't find anything, it was clear he'd left in a hurry. It had been empty some days, as milk in the fridge had turned sour and was solid.

The police had taken possession of an Austin Mini Cooper that belonged to Roy and on the arrest of Mr Robert Pelham on 23 August they also took his Brabham Ford formula junior racing car. However, Roy made no attempt to get either back from them.

Roy wasn't on the run for long because on 10 December officers went to his flat in Ryders Terrace. The door was knocked by a WDC (but in his deposition DCS Butler said he knocked the door) but no one answered. However, there were signs that someone was on the premises, so an entrance was forced just in time to see the back of Roy disappear through a fanlight window onto the roof, carrying a holdall. He was chased over the roofs and eventually jumped into the back garden of another house, where a police officer was waiting for him; he was detained. He denied all knowledge of the holdall he'd been carrying. He was known to the officers and asked to explain where he was on the night of 7/8 August, but denied he'd been to Leatherslade Farm. He was arrested and cautioned. In the meantime the holdall, which had landed next to him in the garden, had been examined but Roy refused to say anything about it. Later he was searched. In his personal possession was £131 10*s*. In the holdall was £12,041. The numbers of two £5 notes found in his possession matched two of the notes reported stolen from the train.

*

As to the three men who were never brought to book for the crime, one wonders about the Great Dover Street phone box deposit. A phone call was received at Scotland Yard telling the detectives that two sacks full of money were going to be placed in a phone box in Great Dover Street within five minutes – the time of the call was about 6.30 p.m. This was to become a major source of intrigue throughout the story, but turning the clock back fifty years it isn't difficult to see a possible reason for this drop being made the way it was.

There are several sides to the story, some right and some wrong – and there are several tellers of the story, one right and the others wrong. As to which is right and which are wrong, we will never know.

The story was that a phone call was made to Scotland Yard – two senior police officers have claimed they took the call, but at this time a squad was preparing to raid an address in St John's Wood where they thought Roy James was hiding. With the amount of crank calls and such the squad had received it's extraordinary that the two detectives in charge of the operation took it upon themselves to go to the phone box. DCS Butler, we're told, was adamant that the call was a hoax but DCI Williams, his number two, was adamant the call was genuine.

So as the squad were planning the arrest of a major robber, the two detectives leading the hunt go off on what one feels is a hoax. This seems strange because if DCI Williams had convinced DCS Butler the matter wasn't a hoax then why didn't they send a couple of their team – at least one junior detective was in the office at the time – or even uniformed police in a squad car to investigate and report back? The press were told that no less than five squad cars attended the scene, so the press who were not there say one thing and DCI Williams who was there says something else! And so does the junior detective in the office when the call was taken!

But the plot thickens because, according to DCI Williams, in the middle of planning to corner Roy James, DCS Butler and DCI Williams depart Scotland Yard in DCS Butler's mini. They go to the phone box and, lo and behold, there are two bags tied up all ready and waiting for them, or so it was said. And things depart further from normal police routine when the two detectives take the bags and bundle them into the back of DCS Butler's car. Then they sit and wait to see if anyone who was watching them would show themselves. Meantime, a fugitive called Roy James was no doubt enjoying the early evening television.

A phone box to make a drop of £50,000? What makes it more bizarre is that few people had their own phone in those days and phone boxes were well used. It is unusual to see a queue outside a phone box now, but it was common in those days.

Another angle of consideration is that two detectives are arguing in their office that 'fifty grand' is to be placed in a phone box in five minutes, and by the time DCI Williams wins the argument the five minutes are up. In those days traffic in London moved at an average speed of 10–15 mph, so even if a multiplication of this is considered, then from the time of the call to the time of the officers' arrival, by the time they'd left their office – the lift wasn't working so they needed to run down several flights of stairs – and got to DCS Butler's car and driven the distance the bare minimum would be fifteen minutes. So why didn't they send a squad car?

If anyone had entered that phone box and investigated then they would have dialled 999; the whole country was looking out for unusual occurrences and the bag drop in Dorking Woods had been well publicised. But this was the official line, that in the middle of their preparations to find Roy James they still went on what could have been a hoax chase. Plausibility for the official line tends to sag slightly.

One would expect that phone box, in a short time, to be crawling with Scene of Crime officers, Fingerprint officers and the whole lot. But the two senior detectives went swanning off back to Scotland Yard with the two sacks in the car. The following morning, after a press conference, Cmdr Hatherill insisted the phone box be dusted for fingerprints.

But going back to the timing of this whole charade; I put them at the phone box at about 6.50 p.m. They load the sacks and then wait for a few minutes to see if anyone is going to show themselves; it was DCI Williams who said they waited. But to no avail – let's say the time is now 7.00 p.m. So they go back to the office, which might take ten minutes; 7.10 p.m. They unload the sacks and take them to the office: 'We found the lifts were not working and we had to carry the very heavy sacks up several flights of stairs by humping them up step after step.'

So would they have arrived back in the office by about 7.20 p.m.? Then they opened the sacks – or sack according to DS Slipper – and counted the money, although very approximately. So would it be fair to say they left the office then to chase Roy James by 7.40 p.m.? But then the two detectives had to go to Albany Street police station first, to brief the forty-odd officers who were to surround Roy's flat. So a ten-minute journey and a fifteen-minute briefing, to make sure each officer knew his position, and then into cars and off to Ryder's Terrace.

At Ryder's Terrace, 'it took some time for all the officers to move quietly into position'. So they might have arrived at about 8.05 p.m. and perhaps taken ten minutes or so to get into position. So, say it's about 8.15 p.m. when they knock on the door. The reason I break the time down is that DCS Butler timed the knock on Roy's door as 7.40 p.m. and later that evening DSupt Fewtrell was told they arrested Roy at 7.40 p.m. This might sound as though it's just a misunderstanding over times, but on the other hand DCS Butler and DCI Williams had acted in a bizarre way and at odds with the proper procedure for the collection of evidence in what they did at the phone box that evening, so the timing as I have approximated it suggests there was more to that evening's activities than has been recorded.

But the press released the story as, '£50,000 found in a phone box'.

DSupt Fewtrell in Bucks Police HQ said just how the police at Scotland Yard knew so quickly it was that amount he could 'never fathom'. With the timing of the arrest of Roy and what the press were told, plausibility for the official line regarding the money in the phone box sags a bit more.

After DCS Butler's death, DCI Williams said he didn't ever know how much of the circumstances of the drop DCS Butler had told the senior officers, DCS Millen and Cmdr Hatherill.

And then there's another point. DCI Williams, in his memoirs (which might be more reliable than the official record, if one was ever made), said that when they got back to the office and he turned the sacks upside down, out fell bundles of 'English, Irish and Scottish £5 notes and of English and Scottish £1 notes'. But the detective sergeant in the office, who also wrote an account of the drop, later said a 'sack full of £1 notes'. If they found two sacks then why does the description later become 'a sack full'? And if the sacks (two) contained 'English, Irish and Scottish £5 notes and English and Scottish £1 notes', then why was it observed the recovery was of a 'sack full of £1 notes'? With this change in the 'script', the official line of that evening's activities continues to sag in plausibility.

So the whole pantomime is played out from about 6.30 p.m. for a drive out, a slight pause to see if anyone comes along and then a drive back to Scotland Yard. Then hump the bags up to the squad office. At this point they can cut the bags open and confirm the story of money therein. It's not possible to be sure of how far the clock has moved on by this time, but if Roy James was arrested at 7.40 p.m., or shortly after, then plausibility for the official line of that evening's activities can't really sag any further.

In time, though, another story emerged, and that was that the money was a pay-off. The story was that one of the three robbers never convicted was told that if he sacrificed £50,000 of his 'whack' then he wouldn't be sought as the police had no evidence they could use against him. Negotiations went on between a senior Flying Squad officer and one of his contacts; the officer was said to be DCI Williams and the contact was Fred Foreman, a close associate of the robbers. Fred said he knew and trusted DCI Williams, and a meeting was arranged for the money to be handed over. With a big question mark hanging over the plausibility of the official line, this story does hold up to analysis. Thereafter the whole pantomime of the Great Dover Street phone box was created for the press, and perhaps others. And by the time DCI Williams published his memoirs the only other detective with him in Great Dover Street that night, DCS Butler, was dead.

But was there yet more to it? Another drop for another robber was arranged but this fell through as DCI Williams couldn't take the money, or wouldn't take the money. There was then the suggestion that another £10,000 had been added as a pay-off left in the phone box for a third party. This is where it gets a bit vague, but the story went that DCI Williams sent the whole £60,000 for evidence to the Bucks Police HQ. But Mr Fewtrell's records say it was £47,245. So what happened to the other £10,000? (The difference between £47,245 and £50,000 is not difficult to imagine as simply being down to a missing package of fivers.)

DS Read, who was a member of the Flying Squad, said some years later that the relationship between Fred Foreman and DCI Williams was 'unhealthy', and other officers were not comfortable with DCI Williams's methods of policing, which took him too close to the villains. Something was going on: 'Nipper' Read is one of the most respected of officers – but he got very terse with me when I broached the subject of whether DCI Williams was friendly with any of the robbers, and I also asked just how much was left in the phone box (at the same time, I also asked if the evidence against Bill Boal was concocted). I would have expected vague non-committal answers and not the terse reply I got. So one is left wondering just what the story was behind the Great Dover Street drop.

I was also told that there was not £10,000 added to the £50,000 in the phone box but £20,000, making a total of nearly £70,000. So if there was another £10,000 or £20,000 then it would be difficult to explain away what happened to this extra money. If the deal was that the man was left alone by the police then he had to be, because not only had he returned a substantial amount of money to the police, but he may also have given a substantial amount of money to A. N. Other, and it might be in more than one person's interest to keep the identity of A. N. Other quiet.

And there is more to support this unofficial line of the story. The official line is that two senior detectives had just been to a crime scene – if nothing else, the depositor had handled stolen money, which is a crime – and they recovered the money and took it back to DCS Butler's office. Then they went out to 'nick' Roy James. A busy night. One would expect the two senior officers who have just transported 'fifty grand' back to DCS Butler's office to arrange its removal to Aylesbury very quickly – instead Detective Chief Inspector Sidney Bradbury was told to sleep in DCS Butler's office for the night. If the money was taken to Aylesbury then Dr Holden and DCS Ray could get to work on it without delay. So why wasn't the money handed to uniformed officers to take to Aylesbury at once? And DSupt Fewtrell records that the money was received the following day.

Going back to the original call, both DSupt Fewtrell and DCI Williams later quote the call – actually it was taken by neither of them. And when DSupt Fewtrell and DCI Williams quote the call their quotes are significantly different, which suggests that no official records were ever made of two senior police officers recovering that money. In the National Archives I couldn't find any record, but it might have been retained under the Freedom of Information Act, though that would be odd as it shouldn't implicate anyone, but one never knows.

DCI Williams said he took the money to Aylesbury himself the following day. Interesting to see a senior detective acting as courier.

The press said five squad cars attended; DCI Williams carefully catalogues how expected police procedure was severely departed from. The villains say it was a pay-off because the police couldn't get any evidence, with a bribe to ensure they never did. Who the bribe was for is a mystery.

*

With the money in Great Dover Street one has to consider this in relation to the money found in Dorking Woods.

The Great Dover Street drop has emerged in the past few years as a deliberate drop from one of the robbers against whom there was no evidence. I have catalogued above a whole series of related incidents that strongly suggest the origin of the money was known and the police officers were expecting it; some of them, at any rate. Whether there was additional money as a 'bribe' is open to debate but there are far too many questions.

The money in Dorking Woods was quite a different kettle of fish. Comparing the two, the money in Dorking Woods was in cases and Brian Field's fingerprints were found. Moreover, a bill from a hotel in Germany for Herr and Frau Field was also found. But that doesn't mean Brian put the bags there, and he seemed quite unmoved a few days after the bags were found when interviewed at his home by DSupt Fewtrell. One suggestion is that a minder got anxious about the money and dumped it, but one can think of far less obvious ways, especially considering the results if someone happened to walk past and see the dumping. An alternative idea is that it was a plant to incriminate Brian for reasons unknown. The suitcases had disappeared from his office in New Quebec Street and there were no other fingerprints reported on either the cases or the bill from the hotel.

*

The GPO Investigations Branch could finally draw up some kind of detailed list or inventory of what was actually stolen; what was actually in the HVP sacks. In all, 636 packages containing £2,595,997 10*s* had been stolen. However, to satisfy the rules of evidence a huge number of people would need to attend court and swear an oath to give evidence so that the details could be 'proved'. The practicality of this was questionable so it was decided that no specific amount of money should be stated, but that the stolen property should be shown as 120 mailbags.

18

MANAGING THE ENQUIRY

Right from the start the police realised the crime was big, and it was decided that all operations would be co-ordinated from Bucks Police HQ in Aylesbury, which was about 10 miles from the scene. The headquarters was new, with modern amenities, and an incident room was set up.

Initially, the incident room was under the charge of DS Pritchard with assistance from the Bucks Police establishment and secretarial support.

On the day Leatherslade Farm was discovered Comdr Hatherill and DCS Millen were at Aylesbury discussing progress with DSupt McArthur and DSupt Fewtrell. Comdr Hatherill thought more staff were required in the incident room and arranged for a detective inspector, two detective sergeants and a detective constable of the Metropolitan Police to temporarily join the staff. They arrived on 13 August and the detective inspector became responsible for managing the incident room.

The incident room provided a focal point for the other organisations involved with the investigation: New Scotland Yard when their incident room was closed, other police forces, the GPO Investigations Branch and British Transport Police; the latter two actually seconded officers to the incident room team.

In keeping with the reality of police work a lot of the routine work was dull and repetitive but necessary. Correspondence was dealt with from other forces, the public and any 'crank' mail.

Later on, the needs of witnesses and court were managed from here, as well as the continuing investigations for the suspects still at large.

Files of the known associates of the arrested suspects were also on hand and a direct line with the Criminal Records Office was maintained for the trial. A liaison officer was based in the incident room during the trial and there was also a police/court 'runner'.

*

The exhibits officer started to collect exhibits at the scene of the robbery and thereafter from a number of places. It was in the interests of efficiency for the one officer to oversee this and records were kept of what, when and where found.

The articles were in constant demand by the officers in charge of the case, and the exhibit officer knew exactly what he had and where it was. There was a growing index of the exhibits and it was felt better to record each article rather than list a number of different articles under one reference heading. By the time of the committal proceedings at the Magistrates' Court there were well over 1,000 articles.

19
COMMITTAL PROCEEDINGS

The crime took place in Buckinghamshire so that is where the crime was to be tried. Some effort was made to take the case to the Central Criminal Court, the Old Bailey, but this was resisted. It has been argued that the jury would be less likely to be influenced in the less cosmopolitan area though this cannot be demonstrated. Facilities were more suitable at the Old Bailey but it was decided to convert the Council Chamber into a court and the necessary ante-rooms were made available. A special dock, with ornate and symbolic black spikes mounted on it, and a witness box were constructed. There was accommodation for about thirty members of the public.

Aylesbury Prison would be used instead of Bedford, although it was neither a remand nor top-security prison. Bucks Police patrolled the prison each day. A police officer with a dog was also on hand during exercise periods on each of the days the prisoners were not before the court.

Prisoners had to make two journeys to and from court each day, so security was high. A van, specially constructed to convey fourteen prisoners, was obtained from the Metropolitan Police. The construction of the van enabled one prisoner to be handled at a time. A double escort was provided for each prisoner, and the same two constables were in charge of the same prisoner throughout the day, identified to the escort supervisor in the morning.

The committal proceedings were to last for nineteen days.

On 2 December, all the prisoners arrested appeared before the Linslade Magistrates at Aylesbury. Mr Howard Sabin, for the prosecution, addressed the bench. He said the prosecution had decided not to ask them to commit Mary Manson for trial for receiving, or on any other charge. He spoke of her connection with Bruce Reynolds. He added that it would be unfair for the prosecution to ask the bench to regard Mr Reynolds as any other than the person with whom she went to the Chequered Flag Car Showrooms to purchase a motor car. No evidence had yet been produced to connect Mr Reynolds with the crime. Bearing that in mind, Mr Sabin said that he couldn't see that there was a case for Mrs Manson to answer. He concluded his address by asking for all the other accused to be committed for trial on the charges that had been listed and produced to the court.

Mr Lewis Hawser QC then submitted that Brian Field had no case to answer on the charge of robbery, and added that the evidence to support the charge of conspiracy was 'thin' and that his client should only be committed for trial for receiving. Mr Sabin, for the prosecution, responded.

Mr John Matthew, representing Charlie Wilson, made a submission asking the court to rule, when they committed Mr Wilson for trial, that they were committing him on the second charge of robbery but that there was no case to answer.

None of the other counsel made any legal submissions, and the submissions that were made were rejected.

Submissions were then formally made by all counsel for the defence for the case to be committed to the Central Criminal Court. The chairman rejected the submissions and committed the prisoners to stand trial at the Buckinghamshire Winter Assizes at Aylesbury on 13 January 1964.

Applications for bail were refused.

Finally, Mr Ellis Lincoln, solicitor, asked that the prisoners be sent to await trial at Brixton Prison, which was also refused.

*

Following the later arrests of John Daly on 3 December and Roy James on 10 December 1963, both appeared before the magistrates at Linslade. They were remanded in custody until 27

December, when they were again remanded until 31 December. Then committal proceedings commenced at a special sitting of the Linslade Magistrates at Leighton Buzzard. Part of the prosecution evidence was given and both John and Roy were further remanded in custody. On 3 January 1964, when the prosecution evidence was completed, the two prisoners were committed to stand trial at the Buckinghamshire Winter Assizes.

20
THE TRIAL

On 20 January 1964, all prisoners appeared at the Buckinghamshire Winter Assizes, at Aylesbury, before Mr Justice Edmund Davies.

The first indictments were for conspiracy to stop and rob the mail train, and second were indictments for robbery. Then there were the prisoners charged with receiving various sums of money.

Counsel for the prosecution were Mr Arthur James QC; Mr Niall MacDermot QC; Mr Howard Sabin; and Mr John Fennell.

Each prisoner was asked to plead. With the exception of Roger Cordrey all pleaded not guilty. Roger pleaded guilty to conspiracy to stop a mail train, and on the counts in which he was charged with receiving money. He pleaded not guilty to robbery with aggravation. Roger's pleas were accepted by the prosecution and he was returned to custody to await sentence.

A jury was then sworn. The trial ran from 20 January and verdicts were reached on 26 March on all apart from Ronnie Biggs, who was to be re-tried due to a policeman saying in evidence that Ronnie had been to prison.

*

In those days the collection of evidence, particularly witness evidence, was different from what it is today. However, there are still Judges' Rules, which give the judge the discretion to decide what evidence can be properly submitted and what the jury can hear and what evidence cannot be admitted, which is what they shouldn't hear. Among other things, the judge and counsel are on the lookout for any evidence collected that doesn't conform to Judges' Rules. For example, for evidence from suspect interviews to be admitted a proper caution must be given that the evidence collected might be used in evidence, which really warns the prisoner that he should say nothing which may incriminate him – not so common in the last century but it has happened. However, before the Police and Criminal Evidence Act in the 1980s it wasn't unheard of for police officers to claim the suspect had said something before a caution – such as in the back of a police car on the way to a police station. This isn't hearsay, because it came directly from the person who has heard it and not from a third party – if a police officer made a statement or a deposition to say the prisoner said something, then that could become evidence. It may well be the prisoner did confess, but it also gave the opportunity for police officers to claim the prisoner said something when, actually, they didn't. I discussed this earlier in the passage on Bill Boal, and its practice was said to be common in the 1960s; it was called 'verballing'. Another good example was that against Charlie Wilson, which I describe later.

*

It has been said that it was a show trial, but that cannot be demonstrated unless someone wishes to laboriously go through the trial transcript and all the evidence, which would be a huge undertaking.

By and large the trial was unremarkable and there are few instances worth noting.

Mr James for the prosecution started his opening speech on 20 January and finished on 22 January, when the evidence for the prosecution began. All was well until 28 January, when DCI Vibart was giving evidence about the questioning of Gordon Goody at Leicester. Mr Sebag Shaw QC wished to make a submission in the absence of the jury, to which Mr Justice Edmund Davies agreed and the jury retired. When DCI Vibart saw Gordon at Leicester he was in custody and should have been cautioned before being questioned, so any statements he made after that time were inadmissible in evidence. After arguments, Mr Justice Edmund Davies refused to admit the evidence.

On 31 January, Detective Inspector Harry Tappin was giving evidence when Mr Michael Argyle QC, for Lennie Field, asked to make a submission in the absence of the jury. Mr Justice Edmund Davies agreed. The issue raised was that evidence given earlier by DCS Butler was not in conformity with Judges' Rules because his client had been in custody and hadn't been cautioned. Mr Justice Edmund Davies ruled that the oral evidence, up to when Mr Field was put into the detention room at Cannon Row police station, would be admitted. But the written evidence should not.

The jury returned, and so it went on.

On 6 February, DI Morris, of the Surrey Police, gave evidence of an interview he had with Ronnie Biggs. He quoted Ronnie: 'I knew Reynolds some years ago. I met him when we did time together.'

At the conclusion of DI Morris's evidence he was cross-examined by Mr Wilfred Fordham, who, afterwards, in the absence of the jury, asked Mr Justice Edmund Davies to discharge Ronnie without a verdict from the jury – the fact that they had heard he had a criminal record meant they might be prejudiced against him. Mr Justice Edmund Davies acquiesced and Ronnie was to be tried later. Not surprisingly, bail was refused.

As the trial continued, Mr John Mathew, for Charlie Wilson, submitted that he objected to the questioning of his client, by DCS Butler, without caution, which DCS Butler thought wasn't needed as he was already in custody.

But it is unwritten evidence that in the case of Charlie Wilson shows, yet again, how the police collected evidence in those days, and they did not adhere to the law. As described above, this was verballing (and mainly in the interests of chronology I have left it until this point) but this is a classic example.

Charlie was taken to Cannon Row police station, where he allegedly said that even though he had been arrested, the police wouldn't make it 'stick' because they wouldn't find 'the poppy' – poppy referred to money. So this, the police asserted, was tantamount to a confession.

His counsel, Mr Mathew, had been instructed that Charlie hadn't said this and so he wished to raise this in the cross-examination of DCS Butler, and some of this cross-examination took place in the absence of the jury. When he did start his cross-examination, Mr Mathew started to move in on the fact that DCS Butler's evidence had to be identical to the other officers' evidence – without the slightest discrepancy; any discrepancy might suggest the evidence had been a story concocted by the officers. And it seemed the evidence wasn't what it should have been. One officer said the interview had taken place in the charge room and one said it had taken place in the cells.

Mr Mathew went on to cross-examine DCI Bradbury. Mr Justice Edmund Davies then heard the bluff of the evidence being a typing error, and so he wanted to know how this came about.

In the finish, Mr Justice Edmund Davies ruled the evidence as inadmissible. One might have hoped the two officers had rehearsed their lines more carefully. The jury had been absent during this little drama, so after it finished, they returned to court.

The case of the prosecution was concluded in the second week of February. The jury then retired while submissions were made by various defence counsel of no case to answer on some of the counts against their clients.

A submission was made by Mr Mathew for Charlie Wilson that he had no case to answer. He argued that the only evidence against Charlie was that three fingerprints of his were found at the farm. The evidence against him of his denial of ever visiting the farm had been earlier ruled as inadmissible and therefore the Crown were put in the unenviable position of having to rely solely upon the evidence of the fingerprints at the farm with no explanation as to how or, more to the point, when they got there.

It was argued that Tommy Wisbey had no case to answer. Counsel argued that there was no evidence of the dates of when the prints had been left in the bathroom at the farm and as both the conspiracy and the robbery were complete by the morning of 8 August, if they had been left there after that date, even in a guilty manner, then his client couldn't be guilty of either conspiracy or robbery. Counsel also said that his client's denial of visiting the farm might have been merely an innocent mistake; he was helping to deliver fruit and vegetables to a farm in Buckinghamshire – it could have been anywhere. For the prosecution, Mr James replied.

A submission was made by Mr Fredman Ashe Lincoln QC for Bob Welch following the same lines, except that he said that there was not one 'tittle' of evidence against his client. Mr James replied to the arguments.

A submission was made for Jim Hussey. Mr Justice Edmund Davies was asked to rule that there was insufficient evidence on the counts of conspiracy and robbery. Mr Hussey's prints, it was argued, were found on the lorry at the farm that had not been proved to have been used in the robbery, and his palm-print could have been put there at any time. Mr James replied.

A submission was made by Mr Walter Raeburn QC for John Daly. He asked Mr Justice Edmund Davies to rule that there was no evidence that amounted to proof against Mr Daly. His client's fingerprints, he said, had been found on a piece from a Monopoly game but there was no proof that he had not played Monopoly at an earlier date before the Monopoly set had been taken to the farm. The prosecution responded, but he was found not guilty on the direction of Mr Justice Edmund Davies.

John Daly left the court and left the limelight. But there is some evidence which didn't go to the jury that the prosecution should have presented, though it would be difficult to prove. Between the robbery and his arrest, John had lost about 3 stone in weight and grown a beard – when police went to a flat in Eaton Square following a line of enquiry that he could be found here, the officer initially didn't recognise him and he gave the name Mr Grant. So he had taken steps to alter his appearance and his identity by giving a false name. Jim Hussey didn't have the opportunity to do this. So, looking at the evidence: both men's fingerprints were found at the farm on moveable objects and they might quite innocently have touched the objects at another time in another place; John had lost weight, had grown a beard and used an assumed name; Jim didn't do any of these things. The result was acquittal for one and thirty years' prison for the other.

I have no doubt, after looking at the case and talking to Jim Hussey, that he was on the train and at the farm and that he was a robber. I didn't speak to John Daly but I'm told he was there on the robbery.

I want to briefly digress again. When John was being interviewed, DCI Williams didn't know his fingerprints had been found on a Monopoly game found at the farm. He later blamed DCS Butler's obsessive secrecy for this, and said that if he'd known this then his questions during interview could have taken a different turn.

However, to return to Aylesbury Winter Assizes.

A submission was made for Roy James that the Crown hadn't proved the money in his possession when he was arrested was stolen, nor did they produce evidence that it was laundered money. The prosecution replied to the argument.

A submission was made by Mr Sebag Shaw QC for Gordon Goody, that he had no case to answer. He argued that so far as the paint found on his shoes was concerned, it didn't connect him physically with Leatherslade Farm, but only with a Land Rover, found there after the robbery. He agreed that the yellow paint at first sight might connect his client with the farm and the lorry, but he said the yellow paint was of a common type and the mineral mixed with it, quartz, was about the most common substance found all over the earth's surface. Therefore he said the yellow paint didn't necessarily connect him with the farm. He asked Mr Justice Edmund Davies to rule that there was insufficient evidence to go to the jury.

Mr Sebag Shaw also referred to the evidence of Charles Alexander, the landlord of the Windmill pub in Blackfriars where Gordon had stayed. Under cross-examination, Mr Alexander said that Gordon's shoes had been at his pub from the end of July until 9 August 1963, and that Gordon had no access to them during that time. Mr Alexander also said that he moved them from one room to another and he had seen that they were free from any paint marks. So sometime after the robbery his shoes were contaminated with paint, and so there was no evidence on which the jury could convict. For the prosecution, Mr James replied.

A submission was made by Mr Hawser for Brian Field that he had no case to answer on the receiving of £100,900, or on conspiracy to obstruct the course of justice. Mr Hawser said there was not sufficient evidence upon which a jury could safely convict because the Crown hadn't established that his client was in possession of the £100,900 or any of the money found in the bags in Dorking Woods. He went on to say that the mere fact that two of his bags were found in Dorking Woods eight days after the robbery was itself insufficient evidence of his having been in possession of them at the time the money was in them and when they were dumped. He then said that if his submission was upheld, the other counts on which he was charged must also go by the board. Mr James replied.

Mr Justice Edmund Davies dismissed all of counsel's submissions except that on behalf of Mr Daly and directed the jury to acquit him. This seemed quite astonishing and I discuss the case of John Daly with the case of Jim Hussey above.

Evidence for the defence was then called. The main pieces of evidence against Tommy Wisbey, Bob Welch and Jim Hussey were fingerprints or palm-prints found at the farm. In the case of Tommy Wisbey it was an impression of his left thumb on the inside of a bath rail that was on the opposite – wall side – of the bath; Bob Welch had left his left palm-print on a Pipkin can of beer; Jim Hussey's right palm-print was on the tailboard of a lorry.

The defence evidence was that of innocent access.

Sadly, even now it sounds like a poor script and in keeping with the overall ambience of a soap opera.

1. £50,000 was found in a phone box. Or was more than £50,000? And was it delivered to the phone box? (John Bailey Collection)

2. The phone box in Great Dover Street at the time of the drop. (Claire Macdonald)

3. The phone box as it is today. (Jim Morris)

4. Locomotive 40326 in 1984 in the process of being scrapped. As D326 it hauled the train on 8 August 1963. (Garry Jackson)

5. Bridego Bridge, the scene of the crime. (John Bailey Collection)

6. Aerial view of Bridge No. 127, Bridego Bridge. (John Bailey Collection)

7. Dwarf distant signal was set to amber and when seen the driver applied his brakes. (John Bailey Collection)

8. Dwarf distant signal close-up. The brakes had been applied by the time the engine passed; the next (home) signal could well be, and appeared to be, red. (John Bailey Collection)

Above: 9. Home signal from top of gantry. Roger set this to appear red and covered the green light. The batteries can be seen at the foot of the ladder and the signal is to the left of the view. Batteries visible. (John Bailey Collection)

Right: 10. Home signal with the glove covering the green light, at the top of the opened box, with batteries clearly in view. The bridge in the background is Sears Crossing. (John Bailey Collection)

11. D326 parcel and high-value package coach at Cheddington station, awaiting fingerprint and forensic examination. (Mirrorpix)

12. The locomotive and first two coaches at Cheddington station. (John Bailey Collection)

13. Police examine the HVP coach at Cheddington station. (Mirrorpix)

14. Inside HVP carriage. The ‘cupboard’ in the middle of the picture was what stood between the gang and the money! (Mirrorpix)

15. Wider view of HVP coach. (Mirrorpix)

16. Frank Dewhurst, postman higher grade, who was in charge of the high-value packets. (Claire Macdonald)

17. DC John Bailey at the scene of the crime. This officer took a number of the pictures featured in this book. (Mirrorpix)

18. John Daly operated the switch on the dwarf distant signal. (John Bailey Collection)

19. The handcuffs that held Jack Mills and David Whitby; cut by the fire brigade and unlocked by the police. (John Bailey Collection)

20. PC Fewtrell would finish his career with a bang. A young Malcolm Fewtrell, who rose to detective superintendent and led the investigation. (Claire Macdonald)

21. Incident Room, Bucks Police HQ. (John Bailey Collection)

22. Inside the Incident Room, Aylesbury. (John Bailey Collection)

23. Cellar of Leatherslade Farm, showing the GPO bags as found by PC Woolley on 13 August. (John Bailey Collection)

24. Leatherslade Farm from the air. (Mirrorpix)

25. Leatherslade Farm. (John Bailey Collection)

26. Leatherslade Farm. (John Bailey Collection)

27. Inside the farm 1: Fireplace with Post Office bags. (John Bailey Collection)

28. Inside the farm 2: Bedding. (John Bailey Collection)

Above: 29. Inside the farm 3: Bedding suitable for several days' stay. (John Bailey Collection)

Right: 30. Inside the farm 4: Cooking/eating utensils. (John Bailey Collection)

Left: 31. Inside the farm 5: Provisions to provide for a long stay. (John Bailey Collection)

Below: 32. Austin lorry at Leatherslade Farm. A unique piece of history – this lorry carried £2.6 million. (John Bailey Collection)

33. Leatherslade Farm: Land Rover in garage. (John Bailey Collection)

34. Leatherslade Farm: Land Rover in shed. (John Bailey Collection)

35. Paint on clutch pedal of Land Rover. This evidence convicted Gordon Goody, but was it genuine? (John Bailey Collection)

36. Bill Boal and children in happier times. It's difficult to decide if Bill was a victim of the crime or a victim of the law. Either way, his kids lost him to a vindictive prison sentence for the same paint, but found on a watch-winder in his jacket. (Tony Boal)

Right: 37. Dr Ian Holden. Almost certainly a good guy – he could only analyse the evidence the police gave him! (John Bailey Collection)

Below: 38. Roger Cordrey bought the Rover to travel to Bournemouth and Bill Boal spent time in the passenger seat. (Mirrorpix)

Left: 39. Jack Mills and David Whitby arrive at court. (John Bailey Collection)

Below: 40. Evidential photograph of money from holdall. (John Bailey Collection)

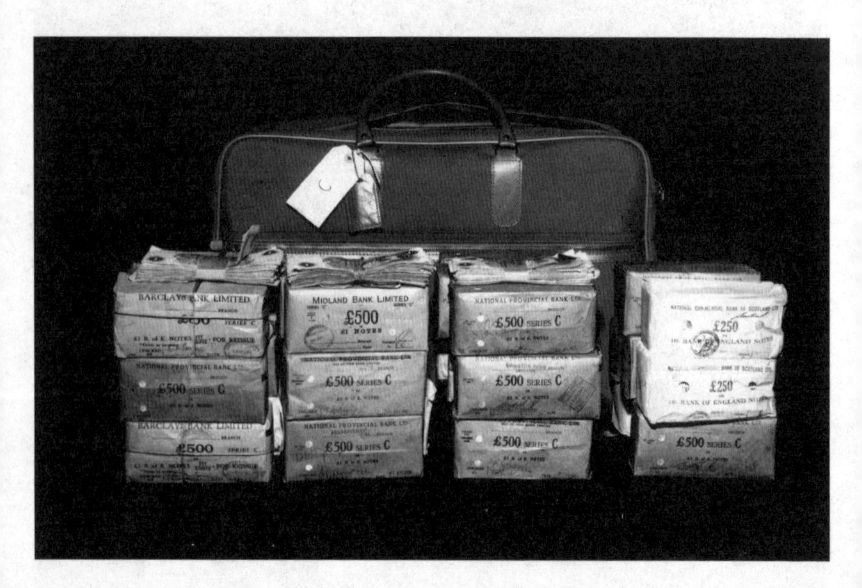

Right: 41. British Railway's instructions to staff regarding security. This booklet was issued to all BR drivers and firemen in the wake of the robbery. (Jim Morris Collection)

Below: 42. A thirty-year one-way journey; the prison van leaves the Council Chamber, which was converted for the trial. The passengers had just been found guilty. (Mirrorpix).

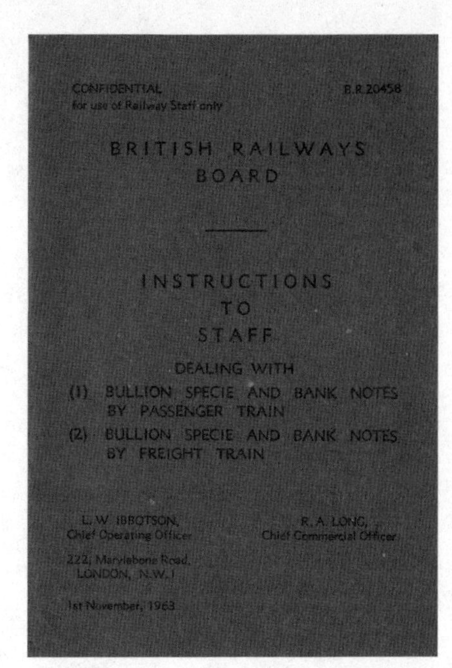

CONFIDENTIAL
for use of Railway Staff only

B.R. 20458

BRITISH RAILWAYS
BOARD

INSTRUCTIONS
TO
STAFF

DEALING WITH

(1) BULLION SPECIE AND BANK NOTES BY PASSENGER TRAIN

(2) BULLION SPECIE AND BANK NOTES BY FREIGHT TRAIN

L. W. IBBOTSON,
Chief Operating Officer

R. A. LONG,
Chief Commercial Officer

222, Marylebone Road,
LONDON, N.W.1

1st November, 1963

PC288 RICHARDS
H/WYC

Confidential

BUCKINGHAMSHIRE CONSTABULARY

TRAIN ROBBERY

For Police use only

Left: 43. Bucks Police pocketbook for officers, with mugshots and details of some of the robbers on the run. (Michael Shaw)

Below: 44. Wandsworth alternative exit: Ronnie Biggs was sprung from Wandsworth and this picture demonstrates how. (Mirrorpix)

Jim Hussey said a friend of his, Ronnie Darke, had to take a lorry to somewhere in Oxford and had asked Jim to come along with him. While they were discussing how he would get back to London, Jim innocently put his hand on the tailboard as he got an apple from the back. At that time, which was lunchtime on Saturday 10 August, Bob Welch, who was in his own car with Tommy Wisbey, arrived on the scene. Jim asked Bob if he would follow Mr Darke in the lorry to where he had to deliver it, and then bring him back. Bob agreed and Tommy went along for the ride. They followed Mr Darke into Oxfordshire where they met a Land Rover and the three vehicles continued on to a house that both Bob Welch and Tommy Wisbey later identified as Leatherslade Farm. On arrival, they unloaded the lorry, which contained fruit and vegetables etc., and the driver of the Land Rover took them into the house where Tommy washed his hands and left his fingerprints on the bath rail. Bob was offered a drink from a Pipkin can of beer but he refused. He did, however, take hold of the can out of curiosity and examine it.

After Tommy and Bob had given their evidence and Jim Hussey was in the witness box confirming it, he was questioned by Mr Justice Edmund Davies about Mr Darke. They had traced Mr Darke, and Mr Ellis Lincoln was to see him in his office. There was an adjournment.

DSupt McArthur intervened and said he too would meet Mr Darke. Mr Lincoln was told that on evidence put before the court, Mr Darke could 'reasonably be believed to be a felon' and that it was Mr Lincoln's duty under common law to take DSupt McArthur with him to meet Mr Darke. He didn't agree at first, but was persuaded.

Mr Darke attended court and gave evidence. In cross-examination, and in light of Mr Lincoln's behaviour and because of the enquiries of DSupt McArthur, it was said that the jury were left in no doubt that Mr Darke was lying.

On 19 February, the defence of Roy James commenced and a number of witnesses were called. Derek Brown, of Chessington, Surrey, said he knew Roy well and was in his company on the night of 7/8 August 1963. He went on to say that he visited him on seven occasions at Aylesbury Prison but that he hadn't discussed the case with him at all, mainly because of the presence of two warders at each visit.

Mr Brown was cross-examined by Mr MacDermot. He admitted that in all he paid seventeen visits.

Following Mr Brown's evidence, the Principal Prison Officer at Aylesbury was called by Mr Justice Edmund Davies to produce the visits book.

The defence of Gordon Goody followed. During the opening speech Mr Shaw said that he would produce evidence to show harassment by the press, particularly by a Mr Ian Buchan of the *Daily Express*. Because of this harassment, Gordon had left home.

On 20 February at 11.30 p.m. Mr Buchan was interviewed by DSupt McArthur with two police officers and a newspaper colleague present. The interview led to a lengthy statement in which he confessed to an agreement with Pat Cooper, who was Gordon's girlfriend, that he would give false evidence on Gordon's behalf. He denied any intention to give the evidence but said that he had agreed to the plan so that he would get a story. At the start of the interview he wasn't cautioned, as it was more important to get the truth respecting his involvement than to consider bringing criminal charges against Mr Buchan.

On 21 February a conference was held with Mr James and the prosecuting team. They supported the decision not to take the statement under caution. Mr Buchan did not give evidence but some of the information in his statement was used in cross-examination of Gordon and some of his witnesses.

The case against Gordon centred around the now infamous paint. There were two different colours of paint and the main thrust of evidence was of yellow paint that was found on a pair of shoes he owned. The paint was traced to Leatherslade Farm and there was a stain of the yellow paint on the clutch pedal of one of the Land Rovers. Gordon gave evidence. He spoke of reporting to Putney police station, on 3 October, with his solicitor, Mr Raymond Brown, and claimed that he asked to try on the shoes and had been refused. As he was cross-examined and Mr MacDermot was putting questions about the shoes, Mr Justice Edmund Davies said,

> One of the ugliest issues in this case is the assertion by Mr Alexander that on 23 August, when Dr Holden came, there were no marks on the shoes. Therefore, the suggestion is implicit that after the shoes were collected somebody had applied khaki paint and somebody had applied yellow paint to those shoes after they got into the hands of the police. There is no bucking that issue. The defence are not as I gather, and let the Crown be warned, withdrawing any suggestion which the jury might like to draw from that evidence of Mr Alexander.

After the cross-examination, Mr Shaw re-examined Gordon at some length, and one of the questions he asked was if he had any idea of how the paint came on the shoes: he had not.

Other witnesses were called and they were followed by Mr Brown, his solicitor, who confirmed the evidence that DCS Butler had refused to allow Gordon to try on the suede shoes and that he hadn't disclosed there was paint on them.

Expert evidence was called, but both witnesses could only say the paint from Gordon's shoes could have come from the same source as the paint in the Land Rover.

The prosecution recalled Dr Holden, who was further examined and was a much more experienced witness, but the general conclusions he gave were that the khaki paints came from the same source, and the yellow paints could have come from the same source.

Dr Holden also asserted that any suggestion that paint had been planted was untrue. That was his opinion but it doesn't account for the lack of any trace of paint on the Land Rover floor which might have got there as Gordon got into the Land Rover or when his foot was not on the clutch but resting on the floor.

On 24 February, Mr Hawser commenced the defence of Brian Field. He agreed that two of the four bags found at Dorking Woods, containing £100,900 of stolen money, were his but claimed that he didn't put the bags there and that he'd lost them some weeks before. A secretary gave evidence to show that Brian had left the two bags in the office of James and Wheater and that the bags went missing from that office prior to the robbery. But this only accounted for two of the bags – one wonders who had access to the other bags.

On 28 February, the defence for Leonard Field was commenced. Mr Argyle called his client straight into the box and Lennie gave evidence all day. The court was adjourned over the weekend.

On 2 March, the trial continued and Lennie was recalled. He had given the matter some thought over the weekend and so told the court that he had lied in his evidence, and that he learnt from Brian Field, on 9 August, that Leatherslade Farm had been used by the gang. He said that Brian Field told him the farm had been bought in his (Leonard Field's) name, that it had been used by the robbers and that he (Leonard Field) would get a considerable sum of money. He went on to say that Brian Field explained that Mr Wheater would take care of everything and see that he (Leonard Field) wasn't involved. When he heard Mr Wheater and Brian Field later deny his identity he was satisfied that they were keeping to their agreement.

After this the court was adjourned for a while. When the court resumed Lennie was further cross-examined, and continued his evidence on 3 March. A number of witnesses were recalled, examined and cross-examined.

Later on 3 March, the defence of John Wheater commenced. Mr Graham Swanwick QC first called witnesses as to Mr Wheater's character. Then he called Mr Wheater to the box, and his evidence related to the purchase of Leatherslade Farm.

Mr John Maris was recalled and gave evidence that he was milking in the cow sheds at the bottom of the lane to Leatherslade Farm on the afternoon of Saturday 10 August, and if a convoy of vehicles, as suggested by Mr Darke and Mr Wisbey and Mr Hussey and Mr Welch, had entered the lane he would have heard them and been so interested as to have looked through the window and seen them. He neither saw nor heard them. He maintained he started the milking at 3.15 p.m. and the defendants had said they arrived just after this. After the trial was over and the heat had died down a private prosecution was brought by Tommy Wisbey's brother that what Mr Maris had said was not true and he had started the milking about a half an hour later, therefore it was quite possible that Mr Darke, Mr Wisbey, Mr Hussey and Mr Welch all arrived at the farm when they said they did. They even hired a private detective to watch him and his routine did seem to be that the cattle were in the shed somewhere between 3.40 and 3.55 p.m. Despite this, the court dismissed the case.

21
NO CHANCE

On Sunday 16 March, a member of the jury received a phone call at his home from a man who said, 'You are a member of the jury and some of my friends are on trial and they are innocent. We will make it worth your while to sway [or swing] it.'

The juror told the man he would have to report the matter. He contacted the police and an effort was made to trace the caller.

This gave the whole legal industry a bit of a problem, because a juror couldn't be approached by police without the consent of the judge. Mr James was contacted for advice but he seemed unsure, so he consulted Mr Justice Edmund Davies. It was arranged through the Under Sheriff that the juror should prepare a note of the incident for the judge.

When the court opened the following morning, Mr Justice Edmund Davies made an announcement in open court and directed that the police take a statement from the juror in the presence of the Clerk to the Court and the Under Sheriff. The attempt to coerce a jury member is a crime known as 'embracery'.

On 17 March, Mr Justice Edmund Davies commenced his summing up. This continued until mid-afternoon on Monday 23 March, when the jury retired. Special accommodation was arranged and a police guard was deployed. At the jury's request a police guard was put on their homes too.

The judge told the jury it would take a few hours to re-convene the court, so if they reached a verdict late in the day, it would be brought to court the following morning. But Mr Justice Edmund

Davies said he wanted to be informed of any verdict at whatever time of day or night.

At 10.30 a.m. on 26 March, the court re-convened and the verdicts were announced. All accused were guilty of conspiracy to rob and robbery.

The prisoners were put back to await sentence.

*

On Wednesday 8 April, the re-trial of Ronnie Biggs commenced. The prosecution case was completed by 10 April.

The defence was that Ronnie went to Leatherslade Farm with a man called Norman Bickers as a caretaker. He was aware that some unlawful activity was afoot but said he didn't quite know what. They arrived at the farm at about 1.30 p.m. on 6 August and stayed until 8 a.m. on 7 August. They helped themselves to food and drink and played Monopoly.

They found Army uniforms stored and if there was to be a raid on an Army depot, Ronnie said they could 'count him out'. At 8.30 a.m. on 7 August they left the farm and went to Oxford. Mr Bickers told Ronnie he had 'counted both of them out' because the farm was to be used in connection with a raid on a mail train, although how he knew this at this point isn't clear. Ronnie had said it was madness and that he was going home. Mr Bickers was said to warn Mr Biggs to keep quiet because the robbers would put any blame for leaks of information on them.

Again, one can find a rather weak excuse for an alibi. Ronnie had actually told his wife he was going to Wiltshire to cut down some trees. Sadly his brother died suddenly and his wife had requested the police search any tree-felling sites in Wiltshire where they would be sure to find him. Of course when they searched Wiltshire they didn't find him.

Ronnie Biggs returned home on 9 August. Mr Argyle said that even though Mr Biggs was at Leatherslade Farm with the idea that an unlawful act was likely to occur, when he found out it was to be the robbery of a mail train he withdrew so was not guilty of either conspiracy or robbery.

On the morning of Monday 13 April, Ronnie went into the witness box to give evidence. During cross-examination he admitted he'd lied to his wife, to a witness called for the prosecution, and to the police. He would lie whenever he needed. Mr Bickers, not surprisingly, failed to attend court to give evidence.

After a short deliberation, the jury returned guilty verdicts for conspiracy to rob and robbery.

*

On 16 April, Mr Justice Edmund Davies passed sentence on all prisoners. I shall discuss this further when looking at the appeals.

Roger Cordrey: conspiracy and receiving, twenty years
Bill Boal: conspiracy and robbery, twenty-four years
Charlie Wilson: conspiracy and robbery, thirty years
Ronnie Biggs: conspiracy and robbery, thirty years
Tommy Wisbey: conspiracy and robbery, thirty years
Bob Welch: conspiracy and robbery, thirty years
Jim Hussey: conspiracy and robbery, thirty years
Roy James: conspiracy and robbery, thirty years
Gordon Goody: conspiracy and robbery, thirty years
Brian Field: conspiracy and obstructing justice, twenty-five years
Lennie Field: conspiracy and obstructing justice, twenty-five years
John Wheater: obstructing justice, three years
Martin Harvey: receiving, one year
Walter Smith: receiving, three years
Robert Pelham: receiving, conditional discharge

Roger Cordrey was not guilty of robbery in what appeared to be a plea bargain.

Bill Boal was charged with three counts of receiving but the jury were discharged from giving a verdict.

John Daly was charged with conspiracy and robbery but acquitted on the direction of Mr Justice Edmund Davies.

Roy James was charged with two counts of receiving and the jury were discharged from giving a verdict.

Brian Field was not guilty of robbery and not guilty on a charge of receiving.

Lennie Field was charged with robbery but the jury were discharged from giving a verdict.

John Wheater was not guilty of conspiracy.

Mrs Renee Boal (Bill's wife), Mr Alfred Pilgrim (Roger's brother-in-law), and Mrs May Pilgrim (Roger's sister) and Mrs Patricia Smith were charged with receiving but acquitted by the jury on the direction of Mr Justice Edmund Davies.

22

... THAT'S INTERESTING

As the enquiry and searches in London gathered momentum, serious crime virtually stood still because of the increase in police activity. It was as though no thief wanted to be caught with any sum of money in case it was thought the money came from the train robbery.

*

With such a lot of money available in rewards it was surprising the grapevine didn't yield more than it did.

Before the robbery, the rate of loss of money being transported was quite low, something like £4 per £1,000,000, which meant that the insurance premiums would reflect this; it was about *6d* for each £1,000 carried. But even with this, one bank that lost £500,000 wasn't insured and the others relied on the GPO insurance, which was only for £200 against a registered packet containing many thousands.

So with poor or non-existent insurance, the loss assessors put up the usual reward monies, which were generally a percentage of the total loss and so were well worth anyone's trouble – even the underworld. A private company liaised between the GPO and the insurance companies, and with the usual rate of reward being 10 per cent of the total, they were discussing rewards of nearly £260,000, which in itself was a record. Nevertheless, the announcement was made throughout the media: press, television and radio. The press were central, with the publication of all the reward details set by the loss assessors. No less than 700 separate offers of information were received and passed on to either New Scotland Yard or Aylesbury.

The First Media Crime

I think it was Bruce Reynolds who said that as Vietnam was the first media war, the train robbery was the first media crime. I expect at some future time someone will count up all the words used in newspapers over the past half century and stagger us with just how many have been used on the train robbery. In 1978 I learned for the first time something I should have grasped much earlier: the term the Great Train Robbery was coined by the press; to those concerned in the robbery, it was merely a robbery.

But going back to the morning of 8 August 1963, as soon as the press heard what had happened the media crime-reporting machinery started, and it's difficult to know where it ended, if it ever did.

The Press

From the start, the Bucks Police HQ at Aylesbury was inundated with calls from the press. Telephone lines urgently required for the conducting of police business were continually blocked by incoming press calls and this continued despite extra lines being installed. Press interference reached such an extent that reporters were found wandering around the headquarters building at Aylesbury and finding their way into offices where confidential matters were being dealt with. Investigating officers were continually pursued while making enquiries and often matters appeared in the press which could greatly hamper enquiries. This persisted until DCS Butler was placed in overall charge of the investigation and he restricted their activities. Often information appeared in the press of enquiries being made about suspects in London, which resulted in matters of importance not being freely discussed between investigating officers for fear of information being inadvertently leaked to the press. The result was that on a few occasions police in Aylesbury didn't get information of pending arrests and so didn't know of them until the prisoners arrived there.

On the other hand, the assistance of the press was called upon in a number of instances to publish particulars of persons the police wished to trace and in this they played a positive role.

On the days that followed the robbery, all of the national press covered it. Generally speaking, early press comment was sympathetic to the problems involved in investigating the crime and dealt mainly with reconstructing the robbery, injuries to the train crew and the likely methods by which the monies could be disposed of. Later reports showed sustained police activity, the rewards offered by the assessors and appeals to the public for help, particularly in relation to the type of premises likely to be used as a hideout. Many pieces of information came to light as a result, not least the message from John Maris regarding Leatherslade Farm.

The *Guardian* of 16 August published an article under the heading, 'Textbook example of modern investigation. Police flexibility and speed.'

On 21 August, *The Times* published a similar article under the heading, 'Test Case'.

Attention was drawn to the fact that the train robbery had led to demands for a national Criminal Investigation Department. It went on to say that such demands were not unreasonable, but they had to be examined with caution. The article concluded by saying that if the CID could, in the way that they were then organised, recover most of the money and bring the real offenders to book fairly speedily, then the system as it was would have won the right to leave things as they were. If they failed, it could only be concluded that radical re-appraisals of police organisation were necessary.

However, the front page news in the *Daily Herald* of 17 April 1964 had the headline, 'Did the Yard blunder? Desk men hindered train raid hunt.'

This accused Scotland Yard chiefs in control of policy and administration of being fifty years behind the times. It suggested that at least half the people who conspired to rob the mail train were still free and that, time and time again, detectives were not allowed to make moves they considered vital. Instead they had to carry out the orders of 'armchair policemen' who some detectives claimed were out of touch with modern criminal methods. It claimed that the worst administrative errors were in the lack of co-ordination at Scotland Yard and failure to appreciate the value of the right publicity at the right time. The article went on to say that many times the Flying Squad were working in London without information being passed back to DSupts McArthur and Fewtrell.

23

THE TRAIN ROBBERY APPEALS

The appeals commenced on Monday 6 July 1964 in the Court of Criminal Appeal and were before Mr Justice Widgery, Mr Justice Fenton Atkinson and Mr Justice Lawton.

The first appeals against conviction and sentence were those of Roy James, Charlie Wilson, Ronnie Biggs, Jim Hussey, Tommy Wisbey and Bob Welch.

When discussing the appeals, the judges held that, though none of the raiders were formally identified, the fingerprint evidence found at the farm was sufficient for the trial jury to infer they were plotters who also took part in the raid.

Mr Justice Atkinson had some harsh words to say: 'Last year's £2,500,000 raid was warfare against society and an act of organised banditry touching new depths of lawlessness. In our judgement severe deterrent sentences are necessary to protect the community against these men for a long time.'

The appeals were dismissed.

The next appeal against conviction and sentence was Gordon Goody, sentenced to thirty years' imprisonment. The question about Gordon's acquittal at the Old Bailey the previous year following the £62,000 robbery at Heathrow Airport was discussed.

Mr Justice Lawton said, 'No questions should have been asked about this matter. Still less should Mr MacDermot have asked questions which had the effects of suggesting, even if he did not intend to do so, that Goody had been lucky to be acquitted.' But he went on to say that 'even if the court was satisfied there was such gross impropriety by Mr MacDermot, as to be likely to interfere with the trial, the conviction would not have been set aside'.

So all appeals were dismissed and leave was refused for any appeal to the House of Lords.

Then followed the appeals of the law team: Brian Field, sentenced to twenty-five years' imprisonment and five years' imprisonment for conspiracy to rob and conspiracy to obstruct justice; and Leonard Field, sentenced to twenty-five years' and five years' imprisonment for conspiracy to rob and conspiracy to obstruct justice. The convictions and sentences for conspiracy to rob for both Brian and Lennie were quashed.

Giving judgement, Mr Justice Fenton Atkinson said the trial jury at Aylesbury had acquitted Brian Field of receiving stolen money, even though two bags belonging to him were found full of banknotes at Dorking. So it seems the Appeal Court judges too thought that it was possible that the money may have been put there by someone other than Brian. Who this was, fifty years on, remains a mystery.

Mr Justice Fenton went on to say that the judge at trial said Lennie Field was 'a ready liar at the trial', and was said to have instigated the purchase of Leatherslade Farm. However, it hadn't been proved that he knew of the plot to stop and rob the train, or what Leatherslade Farm was to be used for.

John Wheater, sentenced to three years' imprisonment for conspiracy to obstruct the course of justice, appealed against conviction and sentence. The appeal was dismissed.

Counsel for the three men argued that the maximum sentence for the offence could not be more than two years, but that was also dismissed.

Bill Boal was sentenced to twenty-four years, and his appeal was against conviction and sentence. Mr James for the Crown said the prosecution was now 'unhappy about Mr Boal's case' because scientific evidence at the trial had been inconclusive. Mr James said, 'Looking back on it now, I should have invited the jury not to convict Boal of being one of the actual robbers. If Boal had pleaded not guilty to armed robbery but – like

Cordrey – guilty to receiving £150,000 the prosecution would have accepted the pleas.'

Mr Justice Widgery said, 'Mr Boal's conviction of armed robbery might result in a miscarriage of justice, so the conviction was quashed.' The court then substituted a fourteen-year sentence of imprisonment for conspiracy to rob and for three charges of receiving, Mr Justice Widgery at the same time saying, 'A significant difference in sentence is justified for those who were not the inner-circle plotters.'

They dismissed Bill's appeal against conviction for conspiracy to rob and for receiving. So the man whom Roger Cordrey had called upon to help him find a place to hide his money still faced a fourteen-year sentence.

Roger Cordrey, who pleaded guilty to conspiracy to rob and three charges of receiving, was sentenced to twenty years' imprisonment. He was appealing against sentence only, which was reduced to fourteen years.

Bill didn't conspire and rob but was sentenced to fourteen years – Roger did conspire and rob and he too got fourteen years.

24
ESCAPES

Charlie Wilson

Charlie Wilson was to serve his time initially in HM Prison Birmingham, known as Winson Green. They managed to hold onto him only until 12 August 1964 – just under seventeen weeks.

Charlie had been arrested in Clapham on 22 August and joined his fellow internees at Aylesbury that night. After the trial he arrived in Winson Green Prison, where he was kept in a cell with a light on night and day, with regular checks by his hosts.

At fifty, Mr William Nichols had been a prison officer for less than two years, and was the 'checking screw' on the night of 12 August. It was nice and quiet but three men were closing in; they'd unlocked a main door and two inner doors with duplicate keys when they were confronted by Mr Nicholls. They coshed, bound and gagged him. The three let themselves into the main block and to Charlie's cell door. He thought it was a guard coming in, but it was soon apparent that it was him going out. Now four men, they quickly left the prison.

Mr Nicholls had regained consciousness at just before half-past three, and he'd managed to free himself and raise the alarm. The police arrived soon after. A search revealed that a ladder and plank were propped up against a wall and it was possible that the four men made their way out either through the neighbouring All Saints Hospital and across the hospital grounds under cover of the trees, or along a canal towpath.

Mr Nicholls was sent home after a doctor had examined him, and some very pointed questions were asked of the prison staff, all of whom were interviewed. Nothing was uncovered to suggest help was given from the inside, though the Home Office said it couldn't be ruled out, which prompted an angry response from the Prison Officers Association.

The police were stumped – Charlie's wife, Pat, and their three daughters had sold their house in Clapham and had left no forwarding address, so her whereabouts were unknown. 'No prison will hold him,' she was quoted to have said.

A Mrs Rose Greddon, who lived near the prison, did see a blue Zephyr car and what might have been a taxi on the other side of the road. In the Zephyr were two men and a woman and this was at about three in the morning. She'd been roused by her son and had prepared a drink for him; she went back to bed and a little later the cars were heard to drive away. A car of a similar description was found abandoned on the Leicester to Newark road a few days later, but Charlie Wilson wasn't.

Charlie moved to a couple of safe houses, but his wife and daughters were watched probably closer than he was in Winson Green, so contact with them was not possible.

Mr Ronald Alloway was therefore created, got himself a passport and in the spring of 1965 sailed across to France. Pat joined him with one of their daughters, and with the other two they turned up in the French-speaking town of Rigaud about 30 miles from Montreal in Canada. They had a house built and settled down to life with their cat Fluffy, and two dogs; a nice roomy American car and a nippy Italian car occupied the garage. Charlie was popular with the neighbours, who had no idea of the true identity of 'Ron and Pat Alloway'. 'His wife's a nice girl and kids are just wonderful,' said a neighbour.

But Tommy Butler wasn't resting on his laurels. In January 1968 a member of the Royal Canadian Mounted Police had carefully placed his van with its wheel in a ditch, to give the appearance of an accident. At about ten minutes to nine one morning Charlie dropped his kids off at the bus stop so they could go to school, and the disguised Mountie asked for some help to get his van out of the ditch. Charlie was happy to oblige. Butler and about thirty armed Mounties pounced.

By courtesy of BOAC, Charlie returned to the UK and was whisked off to Parkhurst Prison on the Isle of Wight.

Gordon Goody

Although it's possible that Gordon Goody was planning an escape from Strangeways in Manchester, he may have been waiting to appeal further on the basis of the illegal collecting of evidence. However, later he said he was 'going at the first opportunity'.

He was in contact with solicitors regarding the paint evidence, and it was suggested that he was optimistic that this lawful route would pay dividends. Pat Cooper, his girlfriend, said she was 'stunned' at the news of Gordon's 'plot' to escape and quickly dismissed it.

Ronnie Biggs

Charlie Wilson took leave of Winson Green Prison at three o'clock in the morning on 12 August; less than a year later another top security prison was relieved of four of its inmates – and they went in broad daylight!

It was on Thursday 8 July 1965 that the biggest story of the Great Train Robbery was kicked off, at just about five past three in the afternoon when Ronnie Biggs escaped. He and the train driver were actually considered by the other robbers as a major security risk; five minutes in the hands of Tommy Butler and the train driver could have shopped them all. But Ronnie was inside for a thirty-year stay.

A furniture lorry pulled up against the wall of Wandsworth Prison in south-west London. This vehicle was about 15 feet high and had a trapdoor cut in its roof – and some reports said it contained a hydraulic lift for the extra few feet. Whatever, inside the prison exercise yard, which the lorry parked level with, were a group of prisoners exercising. Two men wearing stocking masks were seen climbing onto the wall and straddling it. Reports were made of a gun or guns but even so the other prisoners inside the exercise yard started to fight with a guard. A rope ladder was dropped down on the prison side of the wall and Ronnie Biggs with three other prisoners, one of whom was scheduled to be sprung with Ronnie, climbed up the ladder to the top of the wall and then jumped down into the furniture lorry. It was as meticulously planned as the robbery itself and it was later divulged that the spring cost many thousands.

Once Ronnie was in the furniture lorry, he descended to ground level and walked to a car ready and waiting for the escape to be completed.

The audacity was on a scale unheard of in the history of Britain's prisons and the 'establishment' turned hysterical. Was nothing going to stop these men? But if they had only paused for thought, then they might have realised that the grapevine in and out of prison is quite an active one and most things can be arranged, providing the necessary amount of money changes hands.

However, it was the making of another record courtesy of the Great Train Robbery. Through Europe, Ronnie went to Australia where Charmian and the kids joined him. Stories about the other robbers came to be overshadowed by Ronnie Biggs and his global tour.

He left Charmian and Australia when things got too hot there in late 1969. The police missed him for a second time when he was holed up in a hotel on the Melbourne outskirts, from where he fled with only the clothes he was wearing.

By 1974 he was in Brazil, where he was arrested. Out goes Detective Superintendent Jack Slipper (a detective sergeant in 1963) to bring him home to Wandsworth. But his Brazilian girlfriend is pregnant and, as a father of a Brazilian child, Ronnie is protected. Back comes DSupt Slipper.

Piers Paul Read suggested that this meeting between DSupt Slipper, Ronnie and Raimunda had no real link to the robbery; it was now 'simply a case of character actors playing out a farce for the public'. But life wasn't rosy for Ronnie and he had to stoop to some quite low and degrading ways to earn enough money to feed his son.

Life went on, the robbers were released, but Ronnie remained pretty much a prisoner of Rio until his kidnap in 1981 and subsequent return to Brazil. He published his autobiography and in 1987 asked for a pardon – the Home Secretary refused.

Years passed with periodic threats to return that came to nothing. Then his health started to decline, and in the late 1990s there was talk of an extradition treaty between Great Britain and Brazil that would see Ronnie sent back. By 1999 he was reported to have had his first stroke, which affected his ability to speak.

I often wondered if Ronnie didn't come back because of the huge sentence that awaited him or because of something or someone from the London underworld. In a programme about the robbers in 1978 his name was broached, which may have taken some of the robbers by surprise and some quite blunt comments were made. Jim Hussey took up the running, though, and said he met Ronnie on remand and thought he 'wasn't a bad bloke'. But he had named names, which was what had caused a problem. Buster chipped in: 'He nicked the old man's money' – that of Stan, the driver.

Ronnie Biggs was brought into the plan late with the unknown quantity of the train driver. For the two firms this was another stretch on their trust of one another, but it was a combination of Bruce's planning, Gordon's leadership and Buster's motivation that saved the day – not to mention the huge amount of money they were going to lift.

Some commentators have said Ronnie was the tea-boy, but Buster dismissed this and said he made dreadful tea. Looking at it from a robber/security point of view then his late arrival in the plot together with 'Old Stan' would mean that if the Flying Squad ever got hold of 'Old Stan', as I discussed above, he would inform without realising he was informing.

25

TWO MORE IN 1966...

On 12 April 1966, after just over two and a half years on the run, Jimmy White was arrested in Littlestone-on-Sea in Kent. DCS Butler took him to Aylesbury, where he was charged.

He'd lived in a block of flats on Grand Parade as Mr Ordinary Bob Lane and a neighbour said he was a 'good, kind man'. Jimmy had left his fingerprints on a jar at the farm, and also a caravan that had belonged to him and had long preceded him into police custody, together with around £30,000 hidden behind a wood panel.

But he had been an efficient member of the gang and any equipment that was needed, he got. He described his life on the run as 'a life of misery'.

In the early days of his fugitive existence, he and his wife had stayed apart, both under the impression that their young son had been with the other. It was a devastating blow when he found that his son was not with his wife, and Jimmy had to resort to threats to get him back. He found that his friends weren't quite so friendly now as 'money parcels' often went missing, and he'd be told that there was a thirty-year sentence hanging over his head.

Jimmy got eighteen years and was relieved that his days on the run were over. But it's a measure of him that he actually risked his freedom on one occasion, taking a woman who had collapsed in the street to a police station; just how many people without cause to worry about their identity would have just walked past? He was also familiar with sailing and boats, which led to him feeling he might volunteer for the Lifeboats.

Jimmy started his criminal career when his invalidity benefit was cut following his Army service and he couldn't find a job. He'd left the Army because of a stomach ulcer: 'I started thieving and I never stopped,' he said.

In December 1966 three of the four people who had helped Jimmy with a hiding place were given jail sentences of four years, two years and nine months – the fourth was bound over.

*

In May 1966 it was reported that Mr Robert Mark, the Chief Constable of Leicester City Police, in whose city Bob Welch and Tommy Wisbey were imprisoned, had given consent for some of his officers to be armed with self-loading rifles; his justification was the firearms used in the breakout of Ronnie Biggs the previous year.

*

Buster Edwards had decided that he was reaching the end of his road and thought about the prospect of giving himself up. Life in Mexico had been fun and an experience, but he knew it couldn't go on forever. He started making plans for his return, but it was the reassurance he'd received when Jimmy White was sentenced that really swung his decision. Buster was also a dedicated family man and at the centre of his world were his wife and daughter – he was said to wonder what would happen to them when the money ran out.

The robbers that had gone on the run, like Jimmy White, Bruce and Buster, would be able to describe life on the run as fine if you still had some of the money, but without it life would be virtually impossible.

According to DCI Williams, Buster flew to Germany and met up with one of DCI Williams's informants. It was at this point that Jimmy White entered the circus, so Buster waited for that trial to be concluded. After the passing of Jimmy into HM Prison, DCI Williams was summoned one night to a house in the Elephant and Castle, where Buster was sitting with a drink. He introduced himself and said he wanted to give himself up. DCI Williams cautioned him and Buster handed him a prepared statement outlining that his role had been to clear up the farm after the robbers had left. He was charged.

On 9 December 1966, he was sentenced to fifteen years.

26

A SOAP OPERA: 1963–2013

It has to be said that the whole story was to become almost a media circus, and there were books, films, television documentaries and magazine articles. Hardly a week went past for almost the rest of the 1960s when the robbery didn't find itself in the newspapers.

The Gentlemen Require Payment was the first of the dramatisations and was a three-part German TV mini-series. Stanley Baker both produced and starred in *Robbery*, for which he hired Peter Yates as director; a fine cast of British actors with Messrs Baker and Yates took the plot close enough to reality to be slammed as showbiz trying to cash in on crime.

St Trinian's and *Crooks in Cloisters* were two attempts at making comedy films from the robbery. The 1960s and 70s were a time when humour was in a transition and the two respective plots put the robbers in a girls' school and a monastery. Neither really raised much of a laugh.

On the documentary front, the available channels were not quite as plentiful as they are today, but both ITV (Granada) and the BBC put together a couple of intelligent documentaries through the long-running *World in Action* and *Man Alive* series. *World in Action* gave an interesting insight into the raid itself, and *Man Alive* looked at how the dust had settled by January 1966. Part of it was to show Gordon's mother travelling to Durham to see him, and how upset she was after the visit.

In early February 1966, a small group of reporters and photographers were allowed access to the secure wing of Durham

Prison to see for themselves what conditions were like. But this missed the point of the isolation and lack of liberty the prisoners faced. This may well have been in response to BBC's *Man Alive* documentary in January, which highlighted the plight of the prisoners and their families; the government responded through the reporters and photographers – the result was a short film by *Inside Story* that was grossly misleading. And I'm not sure that the film showed much of Durham Prison, anyway.

Magazine articles began to appear; Brian Field's wife Karin gave an account for a German magazine and fell pregnant by the writer. John Wheater wrote of his experiences when he left prison.

A couple of the robbers' wives had their stories told by the 'Sundays' and there was some outrage that they were getting a nice cheque while Jack Mills had received little recognition. So a couple of the 'dailies' launched appeals and money poured in, but by this time Mr Mills was virtually a recluse and his wife collected the cheque.

Two long pieces were written for one of the 'Sundays' by the soon-to-retire DSupt Fewtrell of Bucks Police – these were put together to form a book that raised eyebrows with the powers that be as DSupt Fewtrell wrote it while still a serving officer. After his retirement, he toured the country with the story.

Wilfred Fordham was a defence brief married to the journalist Peta Fordham, whose book appeared a couple of years after the robbery. She made it plain she had a soft spot for Gordon Goody that distracted from her work. After Mr Mills's death in 1970, she wrote that Mr Mills had received part of his injury from falling against the sharp edges of the interior of the locomotive cab. One can see this could easily happen, but after her piece the media waited with bated breath for an affidavit, though by the early 1990s, when she died, it was clear this wasn't going to happen. Ms Fordham made a notable gaffe in describing some of the 'minor' robbers as being like George Orwell's character Boxer, the carthorse; the problem being she assigned him to *1984* when he was one of the unsung heroes of *Animal Farm*.

Another retired policeman to hit the bookshelf was (former or ex-) DCI Williams, who catalogued, among other things, the whole dubious tale of himself and DCS Butler attending the phone box in Great Dover Street. It's possible that some of the story was kept under wraps because some police procedures are best carried out in secrecy, but to depart as far as he describes from the expected recording of the collection of evidence lays the whole thing wide open to question.

Other books appeared to deal with Ronnie Biggs's life on the run and his attempted return to the UK with officers from the Metropolitan Police. Some were better than others – Anthony Delano's, for example – but they tended not to show the robbers, Flying Squad or Bucks Police, so are not strictly relevant to this piece.

By the late seventies most of the robbers were out and their collaboration with publishers W. H. Allen, written by Piers Paul Read, appeared in 1978. This was well written but partly a hoax to spice up the story. The hoax was soon uncovered and a useful discussion was created about whether robbers were necessarily bad men.

The late Russell Harty had a collection of the robbers on his show together with Piers Paul Read, but all of this was done just a few months before Charlie and Bruce were due out on parole; why it couldn't have waited a couple of months is a mystery. Russell Harty's show was interesting for the feelings on Ronnie Biggs vented by the robbers, one of the few occasions when they looked likely to betray their thoughts.

'He nicked the old man's money!' cried one. 'He named names,' and 'He broke the code,' cried others. But Jim Hussey distracted criticism – if criticism is the right word. Jim's feelings in 2012 still batted an innings as close as could be allowed to loyalty: 'He just wasn't one of the robbers.' Another robber said Ronnie was 'hated'.

The media made Ronnie the focus of the Great Train Robbery, which is misleading and, with what he has said publicly down through the years, or what he's been quoted to have said, is what made me wonder if his return to the UK was delayed because of members of the police or members of the underworld. This is a curiosity shared by Piers Paul Read.

Man Alive was back with another, longer documentary, with the robbers giving an account of the preparations and the robbery and a later discussion between two retired senior police officers and a writer.

A detective sergeant whose story of the Dover Street drop differs from others published his autobiography in 1981. Jack Slipper eventually rose to detective chief superintendent. His arrest of Ronnie Biggs without jurisdiction in Brazil led to the label 'Slip-up', rather than Slipper of the Yard.

The film *Buster* appeared in 1987, starring Phil Collins, Julie Walters and Larry Lamb.

Bruce Reynolds published his autobiography in 1995, which is actually a fine piece of writing and demonstrates what potential he had.

Subsequently, there have been a number of books and documentaries made of varying quality. Currently, this is one of three books being written for the fiftieth anniversary, and it wouldn't surprise me if there are others.

27

TARGET 1968

By the end of January 1968, Charlie Wilson was back in the UK and was on the 'rock'. He returned to Heathrow and was taken by car with escort to Parkhurst Prison on the Isle of Wight. The Rover he was travelling in was involved in a collision at Cosham in Hampshire, and he was then taken in a police Humber car which only sustained light damage in the five-car incident. One wonders if, as a pedestrian had walked out to cross the road and one of the cars stopping had caused the ensuing shunt, the police thought it was the start of an ambush.

Charlie joined a group of the other train robbers in the maximum-security wing. There were no further escapes.

*

Bruce Reynolds was arrested in November 1968 after returning from Mexico. He had just £3,000 left of his 'whack', but did boast a case of champagne. He'd gone to Torquay in Devon and rented a house once rented by Sid James, the star of *Carry On* and Tony Hancock's former sidekick. He was using the alias Keith Miller, and had fitted into life on the English Riviera. His son was six by this time and had settled well into a local school.

One story suggested that people became suspicious because he paid his milk bill with a £5 note which filtered its way back to Scotland Yard, but this seems unlikely. The police may have known he was back in the country as he'd gone from Mexico to Torquay via London; the precise details probably died with DCS

Butler, but there was talk of a phone call made by an associate of Bruce being traced to Mr Miller in Torquay.

Whatever, one morning in early November at just about 6.00 a.m. the police surrounded the house, and DCS Butler knocked. When his wife, Frances, answered the door, in came the posse; they moved quickly to apprehend him.

'Hello Bruce,' said DCS Butler. 'It's been a long time.'

'C'est la vie,' replied Bruce.

There was talk of a gun and that Bruce was never going to be taken alive, which is not supported by any evidence. Bruce himself said this was false. He later said, 'I had no idea they were coming.'

His funds were running low and any chance of returning to work was slim as thieves didn't want the association and perceived risk of higher sentences if caught. He said he'd reached the end of his tether and was almost relieved when arrested insofar as it was all over.

He was taken to Aylesbury, where he was charged and decided to plead guilty.

In January 1969, Mr Justice Thompson sentenced Bruce to twenty-five years and he knuckled down to prison life – it wasn't a new experience. While inside, divorce papers arrived and were duly signed but his relationship with his wife grew again after his release. With parole and remission, Bruce left prison in June 1978.

28

THE SEVENTIES

Most people learned quite early on that the train driver was coshed. To cosh is to hit someone with something heavy and it's thought Mr Mills was coshed by a length of metal piping. It's also possible he hit his head as he reeled from the attack but this is uncertain – the enclosed space of that type of diesel engine cab did have sharp and uneven contours. Whether he did fall or not is largely academic and the 'he fell' discussion died long ago. Mr Mills was examined about two hours after the attack at the Royal Bucks Hospital. This is part of the deposition of Dr Sayd Masud:

> He had lacerated injuries to the back of the skull and I found one 2 inches long and ½ inch deep, and another one an inch long and ¼ inch deep in front of the right ear. There was another laceration at the back of the skull and [*sic*] inch long and ¼ inch deep and two other smaller lacerations to the skull. I dressed and cleaned the wound and inserted 14 stitches.

So he had three larger lacerations and two smaller ones as well as some bruising. When Mr Mills was overpowered in the cab, two cultures came into contact: Mr Mills and the robbers.

'He wasn't as badly hurt as they said.' This is perfectly true and perfectly false; it depends on one's interpretation of badly. To me it is being hit and pain ensuing, and some kind of shock. But it's on a continuum, and where it falls on that continuum is subjective. To folk for whom violence is more an everyday occurrence, one might consider extensive bruising, broken bones and possible unconsciousness. So both are correct.

*

I wanted to consider the longer-term effects of the injuries on Mr Mills, which I'll do shortly, but it's right to remember that David Whitby, the fireman, was a victim too. This man was in his mid-twenties at the time, and lived with his mum – his dad had died the previous year, at fifty-three. When David was thirty-four, he was still a fireman/second man with British Rail and one Thursday afternoon in January 1972, he finished his shift and went home; he had a heart attack and died.

The five men in the HVP coach also warrant a brief word. None of the men were injured to the degree that they needed treatment on a par with Mr Mills, but one of the Post Office staff was hit with a cosh and at three o'clock in the morning to have a gang of men smash their way into your workplace growling threats and flailing coshes, axes and the like is not an attractive thought. It's unclear if the men were off work for any time but the police, as a matter of course, would have treated them all as suspects and grilled them thoroughly, which wouldn't have helped their recovery from the trauma. The Post Office Investigation Branch would also have followed them up and it has recently been divulged from records that they were on the trail of the so-called Ulsterman for a number of years but no arrests were ever made.

Sometime later, a relative of one of the men who'd been left behind at Sears Crossing on the main portion of the train spoke out to say how it had affected his relative's life – but it was grossly distorted and brought an angry response from Mr Fuggle, the inspector in charge of the TPO that night, who was now in his eighties; he added that some of the five men in the HVP coach didn't work the TPO again.

Frank Dewhurst was the PHG who had the responsibility for the HVPs, and it was reported he had worked on the TPO for about twelve years. After the robbery he was the man who was burdened with the charge sheets as the legal machinery would have to call in dozens of witnesses to prove the money was sent, so for simplicity the charge simply read, 'Stole from Frank Dewhurst.' After all was over, he was promoted to assistant inspector. He had a family but on 30 December 1965 he had a heart attack and died. He was fifty-one.

Thomas Kett lived in Hertfordshire even when he retired in the late seventies. He lived until he was nearly ninety and died in 2003.

Joseph Ware died in October 1996, aged eighty-eight.

John O'Connor married his young lady and settled back into life without disturbance – if he could help it. Now in semi-retirement, he lives in Dagenham in Essex.

Leslie Penn had married Nellie a few years before the robbery. Now long retired, he lives in Chelmsford in Essex.

*

Jack Mills was born in Crewe, Cheshire in 1905 and was the seventeenth child born of William and Sarah. He married Florence Palin in the summer of 1932, and their son John was born in 1940. He worked on the railway for all his life, and clocked up thirty-eight years of service – twenty-three years as a driver – and his health had always been good. After the attack that changed, Mrs Mills said: 'He was never the same man. Those blows changed my Jack. He was in pain, he suffered and finally he died. He never lived a full life after that night.'

John Mills said in an interview that 'from that day on he went downhill. He wasn't my dad of old.' Stephen, his grandson, said, 'He had headaches and other problems, he wasn't himself.'

Without any direct information from them, or from Mr Mills for that matter, it's difficult to really plot his life after the robbery. Most of the reports in newspapers would have been worded to promote the sale of the newspaper, and would be written in such a way as to provoke a feeling in the reader. I wrote to John Mills twice but received no response – it would be wrong to harass, or to write to Stephen Mills behind his back – so all one can do is conjecture. And I understand John Mills is not in the best of health himself. I don't criticise: Mr Mills's family are entitled to their peace and quiet – and this was an entitlement their father and grandfather was never really allowed to enjoy.

Mr and Mrs Mills lived in Newdigate Street in Crewe, which was due to be demolished, and with the proceeds from a public appeal set up by his colleagues and supported by the newspapers, they bought themselves a bungalow; but this didn't happen until several years after the robbery. Mrs Mills said they wanted a house 'with a pleasant view so Jack has something to look at when he sits all day at the window'. This doesn't convey any sense he was enjoying good mental health. Shortly before his death she said, 'He very rarely leaves the house.'

Mr Mills died before he could enjoy the house they'd bought. His death certificate lists bronchial pneumonia and chronic bronchitis as the primary causes of death. Mr Mills had also been diagnosed as having chronic lymphatic leukaemia.

I searched the National Archives in Kew to see if there was any more information as to his health but there are no details that would directly help. One specialist said he had Parkinson's disease, which was based on his hand shaking from the time of the robbery onwards, but this doesn't sound like a typical presentation of Parkinson's disease; this is, however, noted in a letter from British Rail. Peta Fordham apparently offered to pay for a leading neurologist to examine Mr Mills, though he declined – it doesn't sound as though a specialist in neurology made the diagnosis of Parkinson's disease, so one needs to treat this with caution.

In his statement for Bruce Reynolds's trial in January 1969, when he was just under a year away from his death, Mr Mills doesn't mention either Parkinson's disease or the leukaemia. But he does say of the attack and the robbery that 'it has affected my nerves very much'.

Working backwards from this is the trial of Buster Edwards in December 1966, which is just about three years and three months after the attack. Mr Mills gives evidence:

Question: 'Were you off work for about five months?'
Answer: 'Yes.'
Question: 'Did you then go on to shunting work?'
Answer: 'Yes.'
Question: 'Were you ever able to go back to your full driving you had been doing before?'
Answer: 'No.'
Question: 'I think you found that too much for you and you went off sick in November 1965?'
Answer: 'Yes.'
Question: 'Have you been able to work since then?'
Answer: 'No.'
Question: 'You told My Lord and the jury that you were pretty fit up to the date of this matter. What has your general state of health been like since?'
Answer: 'The specialist told me I had got Parkinson's.'
Question: 'We must not have what someone else has told you. What have you felt like?'
Answer: 'Pretty awful.'
Question: Have you been about the same as you are now?'
Answer: 'Yes.'

In the past, a GP or even a consultant (specialist) may have described any number of health problems as 'nerves' and the patient would typically describe their feelings as 'pretty awful'. This doesn't demonstrate anything per se, and it would be difficult to describe any crisis of his health with any degree of accuracy. Even his family would not now be able to give an accurate picture and it's doubtful whether they could have either when he died. This is for a number of reasons, not least of which is the symptoms of 'nerves' often carry a vague description and the effect can be insidious. Mr Mills wasn't one to complain, and suffering in silence was the usual picture of the male.

But just for the sake of this discussion, let me outline broadly what one might expect after a coshing at the time of a robbery. There would be two main areas of injury: the physical and the mental.

The physical pain would ebb as the wounds healed – the stitches would have come out after a week or so and the 'headaches' and 'pain' described by his family wouldn't necessarily be a long-term complication. So after a few weeks one would expect to see the physical injuries begin to heal, but Mrs Mills said he was still in pain, suggesting that the physical manifestations lasted much longer. This might not be the exaggeration some would suggest; it demonstrates the link between his physical health and his mental health.

The manifestations of Mr Mills's mental health would be much more complex and long-term. Even so, in perhaps a year or two anyone who'd been subjected to an armed and brutal attack would start to show signs of recovery – some would be quicker and some slower. But Mr Mills didn't show this, if anything things deteriorated. And one needs to dismiss the idea that he was a good actor, as some have commented.

So we shall consider some possibilities of how it had 'affected [his] nerves very much'.

Any approach to ascertaining a more workable description of his 'nerves' would involve having a look at his life. Questions like 'Do you enjoy … ? Is there any pleasure in … ? What is your sleeping pattern like? Does everything seem a bit of an effort? Do you feel tired and listless a lot of the time? Do you feel sad? Do you feel important anymore? Appetite? Sex drive? Concentration? Do you enjoy visits from your workmates, friends, family etc.?'

Not a bombarding of questions, as the list suggests, but a quiet, gentle approach. As each point was discussed there would be more questions to deal with to build up an impression of how he was living his life. And 'pain' and 'headaches' in this context would be major areas of concern.

None of it is a measure of any weakness or deficit, merely the way a normal, fit person would be expected to be affected. But what would not be a surprise to find in someone in Mr Mills's predicament would be a feeling of dread for some abstract or impending doom, or a feeling like one is living in a black hole where the sun never shines, coupled to feeling helpless, hopeless and worthless – and the feelings are relentless. One feeling feeds on another and the vicious circle is formed; a vicious circle which can often become a downward spiral.

So what makes this a difficult and horribly unique position is that Mr Mills becomes an item of propaganda the 'establishment' can use against the robbers – or anyone who has some kind of secret, or possibly public admiration for this group of bandits. And then come the sentences, moving everything up a notch. The capture of Jimmy White, Buster Edwards and Bruce Reynolds in the years after. The release of the lesser conspirators. The death of the police officers. The selling of the life stories to newspapers. The escapes and the ensuing furore. The list goes on and all the time a once proud and still honourable man isn't living in quiet obscurity, he's being knocked further and further away from the peace and quiet he deserves. If he picked up a newspaper, turned on the television or even went for a walk and met someone he knew or was seen by someone he didn't know there were constant reminders. A constant hammer away; a constant block on him 'putting it behind him'.

To say this is likely to inhibit his recovery from the effects of the robbery on his mental health is a huge understatement. Most of us with this to contend with would want to lock ourselves away from the world. I can't help thinking about what his wife, son and grandson have said. One has to be careful, though, and I can only look at risk factors and discuss things generally, but being a fixed media or propaganda feature is not going to be a happy position.

So if I'm looking at risk factors, then what would someone in Mr Mills's position be at risk of? One thing that doesn't so much spring to mind as leap out at one is depression.

On the subject of returning to work initially:

Question: 'I think you found that too much for you and you went off sick in November 1965?'

Answer: 'Yes.'

This was a job he had done for years, and moreover, he was returning to light duties, but it was still too much. In the original trial he was also quoted to have said, 'My nerves have been terrible since the night I was attacked in my train and hearing these sentences hasn't made them any better. I have not worked since the night of the robbery. I have been too ill to do so.'

Just before his death, Mrs Mills said, 'He very rarely leaves the house.' One cannot say for sure that there was a depressive feature to Mr Mills's health in the final few years of his life, but if there wasn't a depressive element to his mood by then he must have been made of different stuff to the rest of us.

So the robbers, or one of them, started off a chain reaction the media wouldn't let go of. Writing this, I am equally culpable.

One of the reasons I wanted to discuss depression is because there is a strong relationship between depression and the immune system. It can cause an increase in a number of stress hormones like cortisol and adrenalin, which can cause a decrease in the ability of the body to repair itself, and depression can also affect the efficiency of a number of the body's organs. The diagnosis and treatment of depression is therefore helpful in making one function and feel better in the short term, but it can also play an essential part in longer-term health.

Mrs Mills said he 'was in pain'. Pain and depression are very closely linked; pain can exacerbate depression and depression can exacerbate pain. If one is in constant pain, even a minor pain, then over time, the depression can make the pain more severe; thence the depression becomes more severe and then the pain becomes more severe still, and so on. As Orwell put it, 'an effect can become a cause, reinforcing the original cause and producing the same effect in an intensified form, and so on indefinitely'.

Some of the pain might not have had an apparent source and a doctor will say that what is wrong or causing the pain may not be physical. But this is not a case of it being 'all in the mind', because with depression the fatigue is so intense and the normal aches and pains can be magnified by the dynamics between pain and depression, and as I say above, the immune system, which helps fight disease, may be less efficient during depression and so the body is more susceptible.

In Jack Mills's time the medical world was different to the way it is today. These days there is far more understanding and this is reflected in medicine and its allied professions. The drug manufacturers have been active too; new drugs are mild in their side-effects and the frankly dangerous anti-depressants of a generation or so ago are on the decline. Serotonin, a brain chemical so closely allied to depression, pain and sleep, is now thought to be the core of the problem: modern drugs allow the body to use the natural serotonin more efficiently. Replacing serotonin is not desirable; if one is not using the stuff independently, then an increase doesn't lead to greater efficiency.

This is merely a hypothesis, but if there is a hypothetical situation where depression may have been present – and it sounds as though it was more than a possibility – then if this could have been picked up and treated, one can see that his immune system would have functioned better. And there was a flu epidemic in Crewe in the winter of 1969/70 that saw up to 12 per cent of the postal workforce off sick; at a peak 25 per cent of buses didn't run and a couple of the staples at the time, British Rail Engineering and Rolls-Royce, reported 25 per cent of its workers off sick – sickness benefit claims were six times the average in Crewe that winter. One complication of flu, particularly with an individual with a compromised immune system, is pneumonia. And that can and does kill.

Looking at things head-on, Mr Mills caught the flu that winter and was sent to hospital, where he died from bronchial pneumonia; he also had chronic bronchitis. On top of this he had chronic lymphatic leukaemia, but the leukaemia was unlikely to have had a bearing on his death, especially that early in the disease process. It was probable his long-term well-being had been slowly eroded, that the pneumonia was more difficult or impossible for him to recover from. This is conjecture, but most established facts start off as a question, and preventative or health promotion questions frequently discuss risk factors.

Leukaemia is a disease of the blood that can also affect the immune system but in the form Mr Mills had, it would have been a slow erosion over many years. Most people consider leukaemia a killer disease, which it can be; it is a cancer of the blood. But like most other illnesses and cancers, it has a number of forms, some of which may well lead to an early death if untreated or undiagnosed. Acute myeloid leukaemia has a rapid onset and can quickly lead to deterioration and death. But one has to say that the treatments available these days are effective and the outcome (prognosis) is often positive. With chronic lymphatic leukaemia, one sees a slow onset and the time span of the illness can be measured in years – or even decades. Leukaemia is not always confined to children, in fact chronic lymphatic leukaemia is more associated with middle age, usually the over-fifties, and tends to affect men more than women.

It's often only diagnosed by pure chance; one might have a blood test, usually for another reason, or there might be some swelling noticed. Often it's just monitored, usually by the patient's GP, as discomfort or pain is minimal before it has really progressed. After this it can be treated quite successfully. Some illnesses are treated symptomatically, which means treatment given is to relieve the pain or discomfort rather than 'curing' the illness.

So it would be true to say that Mr Mills didn't have a severe form of leukaemia and it was in its early stages. Some documentation suggests he was diagnosed somewhere between the winter of 1967 and October 1969, and a comment made in a medical report in late 1969 suggests Mr Mills may have been unaware of the illness – in those days doctors wouldn't tell you things unless you really needed to know – but it does suggest that the physical symptoms or discomfort, the type of things that might take you to your GP in the first place, were minimal, if present at all, and the diagnosis could well have been made because he had a blood test for something else.

So the leukaemia tended to be more of a complication than a primary problem, and the main complication was that it tended to confuse the discussion of his health.

Another topical 'illness' is Post-Traumatic Stress Disorder or Syndrome (PTSD), which has been around for a lot longer than the word formation to describe it. As long ago as the First World War, shell shock was noted and the problem was recognised as a problem in Vietnam War veterans, but a victim of violent crime is equally at risk. Whether it's a 'disorder' or type of illness is a matter of debate as stress or a similar reaction after a painful event is normal and to be expected – but it's when the reaction leads to a set of circumstances that make life before and after the attack take on a stark contrast. There is research at present looking at DNA from people with PTSD and there is some suggestion one's immune system is affected.

Both depression and PTSD can be helped in a number of ways. Drugs do tend to help but only like painkillers after an operation, although treatment may well continue for a number of months. Anti-depressants might give an extra bit of strength to the body to enable it to heal itself.

The concept of counselling is quite sound, but it's not as simple as the term 'talk therapy' suggests. Counselling is a way in which the effects of a trauma can be dealt with and one can move on, but a counsellor is a facilitator and counselling is not treatment where one person does something to another. But this is assuming the problem is willing to let you move on; with the constant media attention and the relentless reporting of the crime and the robbers' antics, this may well have been inhibited in Mr Mills. So it's a prerequisite of counselling that the milieu in which one lives is conducive to recovery without a constant reminder of the trauma.

*

Mr Mills's injuries have been discussed and most people who have looked at the crime know about the controversy. The lawyers have almost certainly discussed the seriousness of the injury, and of all people they would be aware of the distinction between assault, actual bodily harm, grievous bodily harm and so on. But, of course, it might not be in their interest to ever be detached about it; drama is the key word in court. Even Mr Justice Edmund Davies described Mr Mills as 'nerve shattered'.

But it doesn't seem that anyone has taken a minute to consider what the effects this constant use of his injuries would be on Mr Mills. The argument was just to condemn the robbers, despite there being a distinction between assault, actual bodily harm, grievous bodily harm and so on.

The robbers regretted the coshing, but it became about the only thing the 'establishment' could use to condemn them. However, in their eyes it wasn't serious – and they might actually be more right than they thought.

*

Jack Mills was systematically used and abused as the victim of the Great Train Robbery, and whether he liked it or not, his head swathed in bandages became the symbol of the 'evil' of the train robbers, without his consent, and to hell with the other victims. Every time the picture of him with his head in a bandage is shown, and every time that a reference is made to him, even today, nearly fifty years on, if the story is reported one knows the second sentence of the report without even looking: 'Ronnie Biggs goes to the shops. Jack Mills, the driver, was coshed by the gang.'

Jack Mills was always put right in the middle of it. Piers Paul Read said some journalists would 'exhume the corpse of the train driver Mills to weep crocodile tears'. Taking everything as a whole – he was coshed, he was constantly reminded and he tried to withdraw from the unwanted attention. Each day would have become a struggle: his mood would subdue, his pain would exacerbate and depression is therefore inevitable. Depression compromises his immune system, and with a compromised immune system he catches the flu, which soon turns to pneumonia. He dies. There is, therefore, a link between the coshing and his death, but the coshing only started the process.

29

THE TRUTH, THE WHOLE TRUTH & NOTHING BUT THE TRUTH

There were dozens of officers on the case, if not over one hundred, possibly even more if one takes the wider investigations of, say, the follow-up to the sale of Pipkin beer into account. I have highlighted some of the areas of concern with their methods of investigation or in the collection of evidence, and this only relates to a small minority of them. All walks of life will have 'wrong 'uns', even lawyers. It seems as though the lawyers in this case were sound, though Mr MacDermot more than suggested Gordon was lucky to get away with the 'airport job', an allusion for which he was roundly criticised.

But some lawyers see court as a gaming arena and the object is to win; justice seems to come second. In two cases of murder I have written about elsewhere, counsel for the prosecution lied to the jury: one moved the scene of the crime 66 yards to help secure a conviction, and the other asserted that two men sat in a lorry and witnessed an event when it was actually three men – the third man didn't refute the claims of the other two, he simply saw events differently. Other witnesses who saw that lorry said there were three men. This is interesting because in court they lied; they said they only saw two men. Why did they say they only saw two men when they said earlier that they had seen three? The answer would seem to be that that is what the prosecution and the police wanted them to say.

In both of these cases a man was hanged, and in both instances he was almost certainly innocent. So dishonesty is not quite the exclusive 'right' of villains.

*

On the subject of the 'establishment' condemning the robbers, there was an interesting little piece in a newspaper from the *Great Train Robbery Files*. It said, 'Thirty years for train robbing ... a night porter who set fire to a Brighton hotel ... and caused the deaths of seven gets only five years. A man who killed a barmaid by putting cyanide in her beer ... gets the same.'

A young man of eighteen got a job as a night porter in the Marine Hotel in Brighton. There was a wedding party that went on into the early hours, and he was said to have been annoyed at guests who stayed up drinking, so he set light to some curtains and, in the fire that ensued, seven people died. At Essex Assizes in January 1969 he was sentenced to five years – he wasn't detained under the Mental Health Act so was deemed fit to plead – one has to question whether the judge was fit to sentence.

A man was charged with murder when a barmaid died about thirty minutes after he'd put cyanide in her drink. She was drinking Guinness, as was he, and his defence was that he was feeling suicidal and mistook her glass for his. He was convicted of manslaughter, and sentenced to five years.

One has to recognise that both men were not professional criminals, and it is unlikely that they would offend again. Taking Fred West and Harold Shipman and others out of the equation, murderers don't often re-offend – two big success stories of the rehabilitation of killers were Christopher Craig (Derek Bently didn't get a fair trial, but that was because of a dishonest judge) and Mary Bell. But thirty years for a coshing and five years for a killing is an unacceptable imbalance of principles. They put the train robbers away, but to let these two killers out seems to risk our safety rather than our mail. When the Brighton night porter was sentenced he was told he had committed 'a reckless and highly irresponsible act'. I think five years for seven deaths is reckless and irresponsible.

I'm not saying that the robbers were angels, but in the process of researching and speaking to one of the robbers I mentioned the 'taking' of the rail crew, I got a response which surprised me at the time. It was almost a plea for me to believe: 'I didn't hurt him! I didn't hurt him!'

And, of course, the coshing wasn't the only reason the 'authorities' reacted as they did, nor was it the robbery and conspiracy – they were a highly organised gang.

30

LOCOMOTIVE D326

... And the Loss of Money

The locomotive Mr Mills was driving that night had a colourful career, with three major incidents in its twenty-odd-year life.

It was manufactured by English Electric at its Vulcan Foundry at Newton-le-Willows on Merseyside, and introduced to traffic as D326 in December 1960. It was one of a class of 200 that were nearly 70 feet in length and weighed just over 130 tons; top speed was 90 mph.

During the early sixties the transition from steam to diesel and electric power was completed and from the mid-fifties to the mid-sixties a new approach was needed for driver training. Steam drivers like Mr Mills had to relearn their life's work and this couldn't be done gradually; there were only about ten years to retrain all the drivers. Whereas steam drivers had learnt on the job over a number of years, time didn't permit this to happen. The locomotives were more complex, so there was more emphasis on classroom training and management took a bigger role in defining the training needs. If one considers that just after the war, ASLEF, the train drivers' union, had around 70,000 members then one can start to appreciate the size of the task. The other main railway union, the NUR, also had many drivers, including Jack Mills as members. So to retrain such a vast amount was no easy task.

On the subject of driver training, this would be as good a time as any to think about the other man who could have driven the train to Bridego Bridge – the fireman, David Whitby. It has been argued that if the coshing of Mr Mills had been even a slight degree more severe and he had lost consciousness then the robbery wouldn't have happened because the divided train couldn't have been moved. But David Whitby would have been able to drive the train – he was still a fireman but training would have commenced by now.

The train, when left by the robbers at Bridego Bridge, was moved on into Cheddington station by the fireman of another train.

... And the Loss of Life

On Boxing Day 1962, in 'severe weather', Mr John Russell was driving the engine and was at Minshull Vernon just a few miles north of Crewe. The train had been stopped at a red light. Both Mr Russell and the fireman, Victor McCallum, had tried to phone the signalman but got no reply; he thought the line ahead was clear and they should advance to the next signal light, but he'd badly misjudged his speed and crashed into the rear of a train headed for Birmingham. A total of eighteen people died and thirty-four were 'seriously injured' – Mr Russell had passed the red light but had not seen the lamp on the rear of the train in time to stop before crashing. He reported that his speedometer did not register the speed as he was going so slowly, but reports were made of the train travelling between 15 and 22 mph. Mr Russell was held to blame.

... And the Loss of Brakes

On 4 August 1965 Mr David Foster, who was a signalman, was on duty in his signal box on the line between Wolverhampton and Birmingham. On the approach lines to Birmingham's New Street station the engine's vacuum brake system failed and the train reached speeds of up to 50 mph on the approach line. Mr Foster could see a disaster about to happen, so he diverted the train to another line which had a stationary goods train on it – he left his signal box and, equipped with a red flag, managed to warn the crew of the stationary goods train to leave their cab as another train was about to crash. The driver of the train released his brakes to absorb some of the impact but Mr Benjamin Daniels, the guard, received slight injuries.

... And the Loss of Identity

The locomotive was renumbered in the early seventies to 40326. It was withdrawn from service in 1984 and very soon after was cut up at Doncaster works. British Rail didn't linger on this because it was thought souvenir hunters would descend in numbers.

31

OUT! THE LAST TWO DECADES OF THE TWENTIETH CENTURY

Charlie Wilson and Roy James were said to have teamed up together in the early eighties with a plot to defraud Customs and VAT. It centred around the melting of gold coins for resale and not declaring the VAT. The trial didn't really go anywhere and the two didn't go back to prison with a guilty verdict. But there may have been a trade-off, and Charlie made a substantial payment to the VAT collectors.

Roy did go back to prison, as there was a serious incident where he shot his father-in-law and there was some harm to his estranged wife. Roy and his wife had parted, and he had custody of the couple's children but his wife saw them frequently. He was given six years and was in his early sixties when he came out of prison in the late summer of 1997. Roy had heart surgery and was involved in clinical trials; some sources say the trial was for a new drug, but others who were closer to Roy have said it was surgery. As he was recovering he had a heart attack and died aged sixty-two.

Charlie had moved to Spain and it's unclear if his activities were unlawful, but there was little evidence to prove he wasn't on the straight and narrow. There was talk of some activity and some kind of dispute in the criminal fraternity. On 24 April 1990, he was shot dead at his home.

Buster ran a flower stall at Waterloo station for many years. There are a number of stories as to what happened in the last few weeks of his life and the last few hours, but it was reported that his alcohol consumption had taken an unhealthy turn. At the end of November 1994, Buster was found hanged in the lock-up garage he used to store the flowers for his stall. The coroner declined to give a verdict because Buster had so much alcohol in his system that it wouldn't be possible to know what his state of mind had been at the crucial time.

The passing of Charlie, Roy and Buster in this way is said to be down to the whole thing about the train being a curse – a thought shared by many.

*

It was a hallmark of the robbers' status in the underworld that they were a respected bunch merely because they honoured each other by not talking. None of them turned Queen's Evidence and there were no apparent deals done to sell information about each other's roles. This tended to annoy the authorities, but a criminal should be punished only for his misdemeanour and not for his reluctance to help the enquiry. However, there is a difference between not helping the enquiry and deliberately misleading it. The robbers were silent for a lot of years, and even fifty years on there are areas where questions are not answered.

Although any prisoner has a right to remain silent, something that goes back many decades, Mr Justice Edmund Davies hinted at his annoyance at the robbers for exercising a right his law offered them; I might not be doing him justice (no pun intended), but he did address at least Charlie Wilson in this vein.

Their silence, though, is almost an underworld recommendation for anyone wanting a job done. Tommy Wisbey and Jim Hussey were approached by the drugs fraternity to traffic some merchandise, which they did and got caught and were convicted, but from that day on they didn't touch the industry. Bruce Reynolds obtained a conviction also, but he has always denied it.

32

RONNIE BIGGS'S RETURN

Quite a few people have said that the last chapter in the history of the Great Train Robbery was written when Ronnie Biggs was freed from prison in 2009. It was the end of an era, but far from the end of the story. There has been a lot of criticism claiming that Ronnie fooled the establishment to be freed, as he was said to have only a few days to live and pulled the wool over everyone's eyes yet again. This is an exaggeration of the facts and his release would have been on the basis of a number of factors the press has merely speculated on; the Ministry of Justice, as it is now, will not discuss individual cases.

It will never really be known why he chose to come back when he did, and he would have known he would serve some time in prison – his status as a criminal had ceased years before. It was in May 2001 that a private jet owned by one of the 'dailies' landed and Detective Chief Superintendent John Coles boarded the plane and arrested him – even the arrest was covered by the media.

One has to respect the role Bruce Reynolds played in the return also, insofar as he travelled all the way to Brazil to escort him back, but firsts in this history have been the rule and not the exception.

Ronnie was released on 7 August 2009 and wrote a few chapters to bring his life story up to date; the media circus was hot for this too.

There are mixed feelings about this man from police, other robbers and the populace as a whole but he stood out for nearly thirty-five years, longer than his original sentence, as the example that if one steals from the Royal Mail then the punishment will be more severe than if you kill, spy or rape – the whole system is backward and doesn't put people first. If there is one thing the train robbers have demonstrated time and time again it is that money in the trust of the Post Office and belonging to the banks is more valuable than human life and safety.

Of all the robbers, it is only Ronnie Biggs who even came near to running off with another woman, and for the most part the money they stole was not to set up more complex and valuable robberies but to settle down to a less alternative way of life. But the Great Train Robbery did spell the end of criminal activity for some of them.

33
UP TO AND BEYOND THE MILLENNIUM

So what had happened to the robbers, the police and all the rest of them as the new millennium beckoned and started the acceleration towards the fiftieth anniversary? This list is not exhaustive, but does give some idea of how life moved on.

Charlie Wilson
He went to Parkhurst on the Isle of Wight via Winson Green and Canada. He was popular among the other robbers and was said to be a good cook. He was paroled in 1978, but was in the dock again for a VAT fraud centring on the importing of South African Krugerrands, but he wasn't convicted. He later moved to Spain where he was shot dead in April 1990, allegedly because of a drugs-related skirmish, but there is no evidence to substantiate this. He was only in his fifties.

Lord Herbert Edmund-Davies
Throughout the text Mr Justice Edmund Davies has been given the title he preferred. When he was raised to the peerage he double-barrelled his middle and surname so he could extend the 'life' of what had been his title. So instead of Lord Davies he became Lord Edmund-Davies. He went to Court of Appeal, and the House of Lords. He died in December 1992.

Charmian Biggs
Moved from Redhill to a secret location that the media found with little difficulty. Sold her memoirs to the 'Sundays' and later

joined Ronnie in Australia. When his life in Brazil was exposed she divorced him and remained in Australia, where she changed her name to Brent; I thought it had been her maiden name, but that was Powell. She suffered the tragedy of losing her son, Nicholas, in a car crash in 1970, but moved on with her life and even graduated from university.

Brian Field

Was granted parole in 1967, changed his name to Brian Carlton, and disappeared from view. He remarried in 1977, and was referred to as a Publishing Manager but also was reported to work for the Kensington Bookshop. I was unable to discover precisely what it was that he did, but whatever it was he drove a Porsche! His neighbour hinted that he seemed to have a lot of money, but this was all very vague. He and his wife died in a road accident in September 1979; by then he was aged forty-four. Typically Brian, the house he lived in in Kew was Carlton House.

Brenda Field

Brian's first wife, married another Brian in early 1966. Another piece of tragic irony is that she died in the late summer of 1979 too; at forty-five she was just a few months older than her ex-husband.

David Whitby

Continued to work for British Rail. He collapsed and died of a heart attack aged thirty-four in January 1972. John and Florence Mills sent a wreath.

Roy James

The first of those sentenced to thirty years to be paroled, in mid-1975. Roy briefly returned to racing before taking up work as a silversmith. He married Anthea in 1984 and they had two daughters, but later divorced. Roy shot his father-in-law in 1994, for which he was imprisoned for six years. He took the gun from another train robber, who'd acquired it to kill himself and confided this in Roy; not only did he talk him out of it, he also took away the gun. Roy had always disliked violence. Paroled, but he had a heart condition; died of a heart attack in August 1997 aged sixty-two.

Roger Cordrey
Paroled in April 1971 and held down a legitimate job in his sister's florists for the sake of the parole board. Was said to have then dabbled in vaguely dubious and just-about-legal business activities. Last heard of in the West Country, but it has been claimed he moved to Sweden, where his son Chris was a horse trainer and his daughter-in-law was a horse handicapper. Grandson Nicholas is a leading jockey.

Renee Boal
Continued to live in Fulham with her mother and three children. She could only visit Bill in prison about four times a year in the mid-sixties, and then only if National Assistance would pay her fare. But she was a fighter, and had the attitude that 'if I gotta take on a load of cleaning jobs for my kids, then I will'. Reverted to her maiden name of Richbell as she thought this would help her get a job. Renee died of cancer in 1992.

Bill Boal
Although DSupt Fewtrell and DCS Slipper said they were fairly sure Bill hadn't been involved in the original plot and all he'd done was handled Roger Cordrey's stolen money, and although the robbers have openly voiced their feelings of guilt that they couldn't publicly say Bill was not a robber, and although of the train robbers as a whole, only Roger Cordrey ever knew him, he remains officially convicted.

In prison, Bill's health started to deteriorate and reached its nadir when he presented with a history of dizziness, double vision, persistent headaches and vomiting, and he was unable to coordinate his movements. He was being treated for a duodenal ulcer that might date back a bit before this time – this catalogue of symptoms suggests something severe, so it's a mystery why

Bill wasn't quickly referred to a consultant, a specialist. It was a psychotherapist who finally persuaded the prison doctor that something severe was wrong – Renee said she'd known something was amiss for a few months, and he had been in the prison hospital for a month. Speaking later with one of the other robbers who'd needed substantial medical treatment in prison, I discovered medical records were almost always 'mislaid' by the prison, so there is no possibility of really getting to the truth of what happened to Bill. Renee wrote to just about anyone she could think of, all to no avail.

Nevertheless, the symptoms were serious and something should have been done sooner. Bill was admitted to an outside hospital, and a surgeon opened his skull and tried to treat a large tumour but it wasn't possible to save his life – Bill died in hospital on 26 June 1970; he was fifty-six. An inquest was held and Mr Gavin Thurston, the coroner, told the jury at the inquest, 'No doctor is infallible. Failure to make a diagnosis is not evidence of carelessness.' He added that 'whatever happened to Mr Boal, death was inevitable and couldn't have been prevented in the present state of medical knowledge'.

It doesn't sound as though the 'failure to make a diagnosis' would be the central point here, rather the failure to examine the patient, or the failure to refer the patient to a consultant for further advice. For a doctor to fail to examine or to refer on a patient who is clearly ill, and this has been reported by both Renee and the psychotherapist, is careless and if Bill had been in the prison hospital for a month, then this is nothing short of negligent. I don't think the symptoms listed would have been pleasant and the doctor is there to treat, and sometimes, as I said earlier, the doctor might only be able to do this symptomatically, but it doesn't seem as though even this was done. Doctors could be rightly criticised for not treating any patient who is suffering. The doctor might not cure a patient, but he can make life less uncomfortable.

So questions remain – why was it left so long? and why when finally something was done was it because of the 'visiting psychotherapist' saying something was wrong?

In the fullness of time Bill had the same length of sentence as Roger Cordrey – who pleaded guilty. Roger was paroled in April 1971, not all that long after Bill's death; I would have been interested to see if the guilty were to be paroled before the innocent.

Tommy Wisbey

Lives in North London with his wife Rene, who doesn't now enjoy good health. Their daughter Marilyn had a long relationship with Frankie Fraser and published *Gangster's Moll* in 2001. This family was treated appallingly when Tommy was still away; in the late winter/early spring of 1972, their daughter Lorraine was involved in a car crash and died. Tommy and Rene were allowed an extra visit, but even though the prison authorities pushed for it, the Home Secretary refused to allow Tommy leave to attend the funeral. Even Peter Sutcliffe attended his father's funeral. The Home Secretary was Reginald Maudling.

Reginald Maudling

Politician, of sorts. Businessman, of sorts. Was Home Secretary until he was forced to resign because of his association with corrupt architect John Poulson. Mr Maudling had connections with a real estate company in America who saw an executive imprisoned for fraud. He was an associate of Sir Eric Merton Miller, who'd siphoned off funds from his business. Mr Maudling also lobbied for more financial support for building contracts in Malta when John Poulson's company had been awarded some contracts on Mr Maudling's influence in the House. He resigned because his conduct was 'inconsistent with the standards which the House is entitled to expect from its members'.

In our language this means the man was a crook, and had been exposed as one.

It was speculated that Mr Poulson had started a demolition business, obtaining contracts by corruption, to demolish the substandard buildings he'd built in the first place with contracts he'd won by corruption. Mr Maudling left public life and drank himself to death.

Buster Edwards

Left prison and opened his famous flower stall outside of Waterloo station. He returned briefly to Her Majesty's institutions but remained largely on the straight and narrow. A film of his life, or part of it, was released in the late eighties but the major talking point wasn't the film but the fact that the Prince and Princess of Wales were invited to the première – in the event they sent their apologies. Arguments about the train robbers came and went and Buster seemed to return to his life at Waterloo.

In 1994, his life took off in a different direction and no one has ever been sure why. There was talk of his flower stall being moved on and of financial difficulties, or sheer boredom with going straight, though this seemed to take a while to come about. Whatever it was will remain a mystery – Buster was found hanged at the lock-up garage where he stored his flowers. It was said that his drinking had increased but this was about the only 'fact' that seemed common to those who had seen him just before his death. The verdict was left open as there was too much alcohol in his system for him to have made a rational decision to end his life.

John Bailey

Retired from the police and started a photographic business in Aylesbury and took scene of wedding rather than scene of crime photographs. Finally retired and now lives quietly in Aylesbury.

Jack Pritchard

I was unable to discover anything about Jack after the train robbery investigation.

Frank Williams

Someone else who seems to have vanished. He left the police in the early seventies and took up a position with Qantas, the Australian airline, as a security advisor. He published a book in 1973 about the train robbery that had more to do with the police hunt than the robbery itself. He was a guest panellist in a *Man Alive* discussion in the late seventies when the robbers were mostly out on parole, and explained how Buster Edwards had given himself up. DCS Williams finished up his police career with the Murder Squad. He was noted to have been effective with informants and his relationship with some of London's villains may have been misunderstood.

Jim Hussey

Left prison in November 1975 and married Gillian soon after. They had two children. Jim opened a restaurant in Soho called Chaplin's with Gill as the licensee but it didn't last long. He returned to Her Majesty's institutions in 1989 and on release vowed never to offend again. Allegedly made a 'death-bed' confession that it was he who had coshed Mr Mills. This was greeted with some scepticism. He lived quietly in Kent until his death from cancer in autumn 2012.

Bob Welch

Divorced by Pat while he was in prison, he also had an operation on ligaments in his leg, which didn't turn out too well. He's used crutches to get about since that time. He was always a gambler but never returned to crime and his mobility deteriorated. He had two hip replacements that were both in for far longer than they should have been. He married Jean, who'd had a son with him before he went away. They live happily in South London.

Bruce Reynolds

He was paroled in June 1978, now a single man. He said it was tough to adapt to the outside world; in prison he had been 'a somebody' but outside he said he 'was a nobody'. His son had grown up but he had remained on good terms with his ex-wife, and eventually they got back together.

There was a conviction a while later for dealing in amphetamines but he has always denied this was true, and he wouldn't be the first of the train robbers who was 'fitted up' and linked with drugs long after the train robbery – Charlie Wilson was another and Gordon Goody was accused of dabbling in selling cannabis – none of which had any supporting evidence.

He had a few ambitions when he left prison; one of which was to write his autobiography, which was eventually published to generally good reviews. It was a well-written piece with an admirable honesty.

He and his wife Francis, who'd adopted the name Angela some years ago, lived happily and peacefully in Croydon until her death a couple of years before Bruce, who passed away in February 2013.

Gordon Goody

Came out on parole in December 1975 and worked in the furniture business before moving his attention to wholesale vegetables. Said he regretted his lifestyle as he caused grief to his mother. He never married, and finally decided to leave the UK and moved to Spain, though it seems this was a genuine desire for a peaceful life rather than retiring to the 'Costa Del Crime'. Ran a bar for a good many years though it was uncertain what he did later; looking for him to discuss this book, I drew a blank. Jim Hussey said Gordon had been ill in about 2008 and it sounded as though this was respiratory.

Len Woodley

Was in more than one of John Bailey's photographs guarding the train in Cheddington station. He served as a police officer for about thirty years before he retired. Is now a police historian and has published a number of books about Buckinghamshire crime, as well as John Bailey's biography.

John Woolley

Is alive and well and living in Buckinghamshire. The PC who found Leatherslade Farm is long retired from the police. On the day I met him he was booked to give a talk to a local history group – the subject being the Great Train Robbery.

John Daly

Had hidden in a flat in Belgravia for several months, lost a good deal of weight and grown a beard. He was also living under a false name. He is married to Barbara, who was Bruce Reynolds' sister-in-law. John's son was born during the trial so was delighted by Mr Justice Edmund Davies when the jury was told to acquit him – his fingerprints had been found on a Monopoly game, which was a moveable object, but this was similar to other evidence that other robbers were convicted on. Had no money left, so it was said. Moved to Cornwall where he lived peacefully with his wife and family. Had been working, even after his retirement. He died in spring 2013.

Jimmy White
Left prison in April 1975 and moved down to the South Coast. An accomplished sailor, he had intended to sail around the world but his arrest put paid to his plans, much to the relief of Sheree White. Lived, as ever, in quiet anonymity but died in early 2012.

Dr Ian Holden
Head of the Police Forensic Labs and maintained that the integrity of his reports was sound. His almost certainly were, but as for the others... Dr Holden won damages for libel later on in the sixties regarding suggestions that some of the evidence against the robbers had been manufactured.

John Wheater
He was released from prison in February 1966; while inside he and the Law Society went their separate ways. John moved to Harrogate in Yorkshire and it was reported he was to run the family laundry business. He died in 1985.

Jack Slipper
Like the rest of the police team tracking the train robbers, was exposed to media attention, but neither courted it nor shied away from it; he was a jobbing detective sergeant simply pursuing his police business. He did say later in his memoirs that the train robbery investigation was a positive experience in his career and, much later, made a point of saying he thought Bill Boal wasn't closely connected with the crime at all.

He was promoted several times and returned to the Flying Squad as a DCS. Jack was alerted by the press in 1974 that Ronnie Biggs was in Rio, so he travelled to Brazil. He had the bad luck; Ronnie had the good luck as his girlfriend was pregnant.

The fact that he was portrayed as a 'clueless buffoon' in a later TV dramatisation was very unfair; he apparently gained some satisfaction when Ronnie Biggs did return. Apart from saying there might have been a shoot-out at Leatherslade Farm as he thought the robbers had guns, he always seemed a fair and straight copper, which might have been why he recorded the Great Dover Street drop differently – he was kept out of it.

He'd kept active after his final retirement and was a keen golfer. His health began to fail; he was diagnosed with cancer in 1999 but managed to recover from that. As to modern policing, he said he probably wouldn't join the police today as it was 'too political'.

Jack Slipper died in August 2005, aged eighty-one. He'd been married to Annie for fifty-seven years and they had two daughters, and five grandchildren.

Alec Muir

Caused a hell of a stink when he said the robbers were likely to use nuclear weapons to break out of prison, but I was never convinced his tongue wasn't firmly in his cheek. I was lucky too because Durham has a strong old boy network, and it would seem this comment was a ruse to keep the press busy while Gordon, Roy and Tommy left the prison by the back door. But if there was a concern for people's safety – what the train robbers could do was largely unknown – then the comment, coming from where it did, was irresponsible.

The crime had been audacious but the extraction from prison of Charlie Wilson and then Ronnie Biggs was further evidence that the rulebook was being re-written. Prisons weren't as secure in those days – the robbers were about to find out though what the modern prison service had on offer – a new unit in Parkhurst Prison on the Isle of Wight.

But it was when Mr Muir made his declaration of discrete executions a couple of years later that his foot went in it right up to his crotch, and possibly up to his neck. The thought of execution for thieves goes back many hundreds of years and at the time that Mr Muir gave us the benefit of his ... er ... wisdom, the death penalty had been suspended or even abolished. Moreover, the Labour government had introduced suspended sentences and parole; prison wasn't the be-all and end-all of punishments available. He was right to say it was not humane to keep people incarcerated for years on end, but his solution actually suggested breaking the law.

For a chief constable he should have known better. He was a Londoner and joined the Metropolitan Police in 1933. Mr Muir had been a superintendent in the Metropolitan Police when appointed as Chief Constable of Durham in 1950.

He was well respected, I might even say venerated, by the former officer I had contact with from the Durham force, and he pioneered many innovations in his time as well as increasing the establishment of officers. As a diversion for the press, the discussion of nuclear weapons clearly distracted them and he won the day, but discussing capital punishment for thieves in the wake of government penal reforms is hard to equate with common sense. He died in 1997.

Robert Mark

Born in Manchester in 1917, he rose to become one of the most influential police officers of the twentieth century. He became a clerk for a carpet seller when he left school – school wasn't a place where he excelled. But he got bored with carpets and joined the police – his father was disappointed and said that joining the police was 'only one step above going to prison'.

The young PC Mark wasn't a PC for long and he was a detective sergeant when war broke out. He joined up and was commissioned in the Royal Armoured Corps. In 1947, he returned to the police but didn't settle quickly and thought about moving on. A few promotions in only a few years saw his rise to superintendent and he was younger than some of his senior subordinates. He went to the Metropolitan Police but was an 'outsider'; traditionally the Metropolitan Police was staffed by officers specially groomed at the police college in Hendon. It was hierarchical and this needed to be dismantled.

Mr Mark was Chief Constable of the Leicester City Police in the mid-sixties when he gave the order that some of his officers could retain the arms they had been issued with in view of the threat of a couple of the train robbers, who were in Leicester jail, escaping.

Again, one has to look at the political climate to understand Mr Mark's movement, but he was vehemently opposed to the police being allied to any political party and all parties throughout the history of police have courted them. Mr Mark saw this as basically unfair and a way governments could use the police to pursue some unpopular political goals – history has demonstrated his correctness on a number of occasions. When he took over as Commissioner of the Metropolitan Police in 1972, it was only a matter of time before he declared war on the corruption that had permeated for many years.

The new department of A10 was created to investigate corruption in the police. During Mr (and later Sir) Robert Mark's tenure, many hundreds of police officers left the force or were dismissed, with some receiving prison sentences: Commander Drury, who in 1977 was imprisoned for corruption, was in charge of the Flying Squad. So the claim that two protection rackets were active, one with and one without warrant cards, was not altogether fanciful, and that they were in operation during the train robbery era gains credibility.

Whereas Mr Muir was slammed for what he said, Mr Mark said publicly that 'a good police force is one that catches more crooks than it employs'.

Sir Robert Mark died in September 2010.

Tommy Butler

Tommy had to retire from the police – he was on extension when he re-arrested Charlie Wilson – and did so in the winter of 1969/70. Never one to relax unless a cowboy film was on telly, he never married and lived in Fulham with his mother. He refused a £30,000 offer to write his memoirs. He was diagnosed with cancer and died aged fifty-seven in April 1970.

Peter Vibart

Was promoted to detective superintendent and awarded the Queen's Police Medal in 1968. He died aged sixty-two in August 1976.

Bernard Rixon

The forty-two-year-old 'sort of' owner of Leatherslade Farm before it was 'sort of' sold to Lennie Field. He'd moved his family to Reading at the time of the robbery, where he was a sub-postmaster. He died in August 2001.

Lennie Field

Lennie was paroled in May 1967 and promptly dropped out of public view. He married Pauline in 1976. He died in 2005 and was then resident in Fulham.

(Ernest) Malcolm Fewtrell

Retired from the Bucks Police just after the conclusion of the trial, and moved to Swanage in Dorset. He wrote a couple of lengthy articles for a Sunday newspaper that were later published as a book. Mr Fewtrell also spoke to a huge variety of organisations about the crime and the investigation; on one occasion, when he was asked what he would do differently if he were to plan a robbery, he answered this tongue-in-cheek question with a tongue-in-cheek answer. His wife, Anne died in 1989; they had two children and at the time of his death he had seven grandchildren and seven great-grandchildren. He died in November 2005, aged ninety-five, after a severe stroke.

Gerald McArthur

He had a reputation for being straight and honest in the underworld. After the train robbery he formed a group of detectives to look at the protection rackets in London which eventually saw the Richardson gang imprisoned. By this time he was based in Hertfordshire, and one Christmas, it has been noted, this workaholic moved his family into a hotel close to his office so he could spend time with them over the holiday! Breaking up protection rackets was no easy task – witnesses were intimidated and juries nobbled – but DSupt McArthur won through. He was awarded the Queen's Police Medal in 1966, which was followed by an MBE in 1968.

He later headed an investigation that looked at police officers being bribed but also blackmailed. He also headed 'Operation Rat Trap', in which the police actually sealed off exits on a motorway to catch lorry hijackers.

He retired from the Herts Police as assistant chief constable in 1969 and finally retired in 1975. He passed away in July 1996, aged eighty – he was married and had two grown-up daughters.

John Maris

He'd married Grace in 1952 and by the time of the robbery they were well settled and had children. Mr Maris got £18,000 as a reward for his part in the investigation insofar as he was sure the gang were hiding out at Leatherslade Farm. A couple of years after the robbery Tommy Wisbey's brother George took out a private prosecution of perjury on Mr Maris, who claimed he always milked the cows at 4.15 p.m., so if Tommy, Bob and Jim had arrived he would have seen them – after putting a private eye on the job his average time was about thirty-five minutes later, which would have been after Tommy, Bob and Jim had left, so he couldn't have seen them; the perjury case was dismissed. Mr Maris died in November 1992.

Stan Agate

Passed on at some stage but as this was a pseudonym we'll never know. Piers Paul Read tracked him down and in the late seventies he was an old man who'd suffered a couple of strokes. The mere naming of Ronnie Biggs was enough to cause him and his wife some distress.

Ronnie Biggs

Said to have left Leatherslade Farm with his own 'whack' and Stan Agate's 'drink'. The most notorious of the train robbers, and wasn't actually a train robber!

Got thirty years, went to Wandsworth before he was sprung. Went almost everywhere but finished up in Australia. Worked again as a carpenter but had to flee and landed this time in

Brazil. Son, Michael, born in the mid-seventies helped keep him in Brazil.

Returned to UK and spent a few years needlessly in prison. I'm no admirer of Mr Biggs but the way he was treated after his return was as cruel and unnecessary as the way the other robbers were treated.

The Travelling Post Office
Made its last run in 2004, but the Glasgow to Euston Up special stopped in May 1993. After the robbery, officers of the British Transport Police were to travel the TPO as part of their duties. No serious ambush occurred after 8 August 1963.

Leatherslade Farm
Changed hands and identity since that night, and the original house where the gang 'holed up' is no more. There was talk of the place being turned into a themed restaurant but this didn't come about. A public footpath in front of the house was re-routed, which stopped many an interested visitor taking photographs, and so privacy was again enjoyed.

Buckinghamshire Constabulary
In the late sixties merged with others and became the Thames Valley Police.

Great Dover Street
There is still a phone box in the same place, though it's now a nice, cosy, modern example. Any traveller stuck without a mobile will be glad of it to 'phone home'.

The Austin Lorry and Land Rovers
An auction was held of Great Train Robbery artefacts at Measham near Stoke-on-Trent in February 1969, and it was soon realised that Great Train Robbery mementos were going to fetch big prices. A Land Rover that would have been expected to sell second-hand for about £50 went under the hammer and came out at £680; the Austin lorry was sold for about thirty times its

market value. A jacket was sold for £18 and some of the blankets were sold for around £12 each.

The three men who have become known as Frank Munroe, Alf Thomas and Bill Jennings have never been publicly named. Some of the material in the National Archives is closed and exempt from the Freedom of Information Act and in those pages are perhaps details of these three men, but they will not be permitted to enter the public arena until a long time into the future.

34
… AND FINALLY

Wandsworth Prison was described as 'the Hate Factory' and Parkhurst was described as like 'an Edwardian hospital that couldn't afford an architect'.

One has to ask if prison is the right answer for robbers. There are distinctions to be made between simple punishment and incarceration to protect the public, but also there is rehabilitation for the prisoner to live a productive and fruitful life. Perhaps crime can be seen to be part of a continuum, and depending on where our conscience places us will determine just how far we might depart from what is acceptable, and one will make a series of decisions as to what is acceptable. If it is acceptable to take what doesn't belong to us, then does it matter who the owner is and what distress, hardship or annoyance the removal will cause them? If the idea of prison is to protect, then with the train robbers, what precisely was Joe Public being protected from?

When Ronnie Biggs departed from Wandsworth, some of the robbers were placed in solitary confinement, unless this was a coincidence. There are two issues here: firstly, were they punished for Ronnie Biggs's escape? One has to try and find an argument against this, but that's difficult. Secondly, how much of the punishment of the robbers was to send a message to anyone else that crime will be dealt with severely? The whole idea of making an example of someone is to use them as a tool and not think about the individual, the victim or their right to return to society when they have paid their debt or when they have been rehabilitated. Did the country know how to deal with them?

Locking someone up and throwing away the key is far more barbaric than an execution, and the word to describe how the authorities dealt with the train robbers was 'hysteria'. The bill for this hysteria was paid by the public.

Looking at sentencing policy in the pre-parole days, a sentence of over fifteen years was severe. John Mathew, who defended Charlie Wilson, said that the lawyers expected sentences of around eighteen to twenty years but they were all shocked when thirty-year sentences were meted out. Did it send shock waves through the criminal world? That's impossible to answer, but the concept of getting away with a robbery became as important as all the planning that went into it, and one doesn't have to look too far for a thief who became a murderer as a means of escaping. Donald Neilson, the 'Black Panther', is perhaps an extreme example, but an example nevertheless.

Were the prisons in the UK secure enough to hold the men? I don't intend making too much of the remarks discussed earlier by Mr Muir, Chief Constable of Durham. With two of the convicted men escaped by the end of 1965, one has to ask what happened to the others while the nuclear lunacy and hysteria was having its airing, and conclude that the prison service at that time was not adequately equipped. But one has to make a distinction between what the prison service could offer and what the 'authorities' were demanding.

Tommy Wisbey went on hunger strike because of the conditions in Leeds Prison; he was in a cell for twenty-three hours out of twenty-four with a light constantly burning. This light is so that the warders could see him when they checked him every fifteen minutes. There is no evidence that Tommy was planning an escape at this point.

Bob Welch had settled at Shrewsbury Prison and was working on materials for local children with sight difficulties.

In January 1966 Mrs Goody, Gordon's mother, went to visit him in Durham Prison. When she came out after the visit she was visibly shaken and wondered if the regime would affect his mental health, or rather, how long it would be until it did. Tommy Wisbey was moved to Durham Prison, and to guard him,

Gordon and Roy James they had the additional resources of an officer, a sergeant and sixteen men of the 1st Battalion Lancashire Regiment – with bayonets fixed. Jim Hussey told me there was a tank in Liverpool Prison and, considering the above, one might be inclined to believe him.

What seemed a vindictive rather than a proper punishment was only the start, because the 'authorities' were still punishing those robbers in prison because two had escaped; in effect, they were being punished for the Prison Service's failure to prevent the escapes. It is and will always be reasonable for anyone to be punished for breaking the law but I don't think it acceptable that mental torture was used, in fact the idea is repugnant, yet this is what was happening in the UK in the swinging sixties.

It was said in the House of Lords that 'prisons are communities where men have to live, work, eat, walk, and sometimes talk. Although they are under constant supervision this must apply even to the train robbers.'

Questions were also raised in the House of Commons about the men going into solitary confinement after their appeals had been dismissed. The response was that the periods were short, but how can even a short period be justified?

Sociologists will always hope to answer the question as to whether a man becomes a thief because he has little or does he become a thief because society gives him little. And double standards – a thief decides to steal because he is lacking in some kind of moral resource, but a policeman becomes corrupt because the thief corrupts him – is it possible that the same decision process goes on in the 'bent copper' as goes on in the thief, that is to say it is a product of his decision making? One cannot blame thieves or organised crime for corrupting policemen – they chose because temptation attracts them; the same as thieves. I don't know precisely the figures for convictions on 'bent coppers' but they are mercifully low – or does that mean the amount of them caught is low? The fact remains that every copper in every police station in the country has to carry the burden of stigma for his corrupt colleagues, but the powers that be will always blame the thief. Most of the train gang were from the less fashionable (in those days) areas of London and if one wants to look at where near neighbours hold a stark difference in wealth, London is a good example. It is a right for anyone to pass from the less fashionable through to the more fashionable – though the passage has to be lawful, although that's not always the case for big businessmen and politicians. Thou shalt not steal if you are from the lower end of the social scale; thou shalt not get caught if you are from the higher.

But returning to the train gang, why were they banged up in solitary confinement with soldiers' bayonets in their faces? The answer would seem to be that certain individuals were fearful of their jobs – politicians and prison governors mainly. It was not the case that they were fearful for society's protection, and the public feeling that the sentences were too harsh was fuelled in some quarters as men who stole money were treated more severely than child murderers, rapists and spies. When George Blake escaped just how many spies were banged up in solitary? The train robbers took on the very fabric of law and order and some members of the public seemed to want them to win – the authorities couldn't let this happen.

Most people wouldn't harbour strong feelings of admiration for a thief, or should I say a thief's behaviour, but by the mid-seventies corruption in the Metropolitan Police was said to be rife. When Robert Mark left Leicester City Police and became Commissioner of the Metropolitan Police a great many police officers became 'ex' police officers, and quite quickly too. Admiration for the police deteriorated and the corrosion was both internal and external.

Bent politicians were not exactly rare either, though bent politicians who were caught were a rare breed.

At the time of the Great Train Robbery there was plenty of organised crime, and it was said that organised crime corrupted the rest of civilisation. This is an over-simplification, but if one over-simplification is allowed then so must another. Organised crime doesn't necessarily corrupt but as I said above it can lead to the temptation, and once the temptation is there it can only lead to more criminal activity. In the so-called Great Dover Street drop, if the thief was returning £50,000 and there was some truth about an extra amount (£10,000 or £20,000 doesn't matter in this part of the story) then it not only suggests the police were covering themselves with glory by recovering the money, but also that corrupt practices were occurring. In the course of researching this book, I heard of one police officer who offered amnesty to a thief in exchange for a nice new Savile Row suit; I asked if it looked nice and was told that a shirt was added as a sweetener. This officer wasn't corrupted by organised crime, he was taking his own cut of the proceeds and rubbing the noses of Joe Public and PC Reliable in it into the bargain.

What this demonstrates is not that organised crime corrupts, rather the corruption is already there and the bent copper knows where to look; and more to the point he knows where to stop others looking – this is his contribution.

*

What it really comes down to is power; the power that one person can exert over another. Reginald Maudling condemned the robbers, but at the same time lined his pockets with the proceeds of corrupt activities. Jim Callaghan apologised to some of the robbers for the conditions they were held in, but in the next breath said his job would be on the line if they escaped.

I wonder just how many people had more than a fleeting admiration for Ronnie Biggs lifting two fingers at the establishment from the haven of Brazil? He may have been disliked by the robbers themselves, but he did deliver their message.

Over the years the coshing of Jack Mills has been the mainstay of the political argument against the robbers by both politicians and the media. It's true the robbers coshed him, but the severity of the injury, or at any rate its effect, was exacerbated by the incessant media attention and political argument. Jack Mills was as much a prisoner in his own home, taking cover from the media, as the robbers were in prison. The robbers had freedom to look forward to; Jack Mills could only shudder at the thought of the next television programme, book or newspaper, or ill-informed comment about grappling with a gang of armed robbers. There was no Rule 43 – solitary confinement for your own protection – for Mr Mills; he had to sit at home and take it.

The list of victims grew as time went on. Mr Mills was soon followed to the grave by David Whitby, his fireman; Tommy Butler wasn't long after, and Bill Boal died in prison protesting his innocence – but Bill is someone we wouldn't be encouraged to remember. It's beyond the remit of this book to analyse the trial, but it is something I will do eventually if only to satisfy my own curiosity. I am still unable to answer the question of how it is fair that the jury were discharged before they gave a verdict on Bill's charge of receiving, and this was later 'substituted' against the charge of robbery. Forget justice, legal procedure and guilt or innocence; was it right or wrong of the Court of Appeal to say he was innocent of robbery, but to find him guilty of receiving without the charge going to a jury?

I'm told that in order for society to work then one has to have laws and punishments. Most organisations have procedures to deal with misdemeanours by their members, and most of the time a need for training or education is highlighted among the causes – is it possible for lawmakers and penal reformers to learn from this? The short answer is yes, and they probably have, but the stumbling block is the democracy in which we live; the politicians are thinking about votes and not about the public they serve.

But the world was changing in the sixties and the Great Train Robbery may well have helped drive this.

Politically, things were sort of business as usual in the early to mid-sixties. The Profumo scandal started to brew in early 1963 and John Profumo admitted he'd lied to the House and resigned in June. Harold Macmillan's government couldn't survive the fallout and in the general election of October 1963, Harold Wilson's Labour Party came to power. This makes one wonder about the interference in the 'due course of the law' by Parliament that has been hinted at – the thirty-year sentences were reputedly handed down from 'above'. The Home Secretary at the time of the robbery, during the last throes of Harold Macmillan's government, was

Henry Brooke and he was the last Home Secretary to send a prisoner to the gallows. But his greatest gaffe was in 1962 when a twenty-two-year-old woman from Jamaica – who for a first offence for petty larceny (shoplifting £2 worth of goods) and a guilty plea – was sentenced to deportation. Mr Brooke failed to act quickly and she was held for six weeks in Holloway Prison, where she was denied bail and couldn't properly appeal – Mr Brooke's refusal to intervene, his attitude, and the outrage he caused in Parliament made him reflect on his actions and the woman was freed and became a British resident; deportations for such small misdemeanours didn't happen again.

So with Home Secretaries bullying Commonwealth citizens and the Minister for War (Minister for Defence) whoring with the girlfriends of Russian naval attaches, it's no surprise that Harold Wilson's Labour Party came to power in October 1964.

With the suspension of capital punishment and the new, dedicated criminals coming along, penal reform became an urgent need. Mr Wilson didn't seem to waste much time because in 1963, as Leader of the Opposition, he had instigated a study that was to provide the framework for the new Criminal Justice Act of 1967. Among other things under scrutiny were the sentencing practices of courts; suspended sentences were introduced, and movements in other areas such as juvenile offenders and the law on murder – capital punishment had only been suspended by this time.

As well as looking at suspended sentences for crimes that attracted three years or less, the parole system was introduced for offenders who had completed twelve months or one-third of their sentences. Part of the thinking behind this was about the offenders where rehabilitation was 'thought to be redundant' or, in short, career criminals. One can't help thinking that if there was pressure from 'above' for the sentencing of the train robbers then the socialist ideal could see some pressure from 'below', as in the rank-and-file Labour administration, to do something about it. In the event, the train robbers served about twelve years or so, and if John Mathew's feeling was that about twenty years would have been a sound though stiff sentence, then that would be about right, as a prisoner with a twenty-year sentence with remission would be looking at about twelve years, and that was broadly the robbers' average.

But did the heavy sentences act as a deterrent? That is an impossible question to answer, either in short or with the publication of a number of volumes. Punishment is a deterrent only in certain circumstances and most people abide by the law because of their inner discipline anyway. To commit a crime one has to have an intention to commit the crime, and this is where things can fall down and mislead. If one takes the simple example of speeding, then at least three types of offender can easily be identified: the one with the attitude of 'I can control this car, no worries' and the 'I didn't really realise my speed had gone over the limit, I was just going with the flow' and thirdly the 'I will speed if I want to, you'll have to catch me'. These days all three will be fined because they will be trapped by a machine, but the machine cannot differentiate between the reckless, the careless and the downright dangerous. But then it can be said that it's the mere existence of this machine that can act as a deterrent.

So to take things to the other extreme, is hanging a deterrent to murder? To me it isn't – the deterrent is the whole thought of inflicting harm to another; not, I suppose, that different to the vast majority of folk. But thinking about some of the murderers in prison now, the majority are the result of minor matters of conflict that got right out of hand. It's true that some of them may have been fuelled by excessive alcohol or other substances, but at a flashpoint where harm becomes inevitable, it's impossible to measure if the thought of them hanging would have deterred them. Here a lack of evidence and the lack of any possibility to obtain evidence make the question of deterrent impossible to answer.

Prisons are not the perfect answer to crime, but it's difficult to know what is. For professional thieves and criminals it's a place where contacts are made and lessons are learned – but those lessons mainly revolve around honing one's skills in crime and evading detection. For killers it can have a rehabilitative function but not always, and one has to avoid heaping them all up in one pile. Hanging is the State killing a human being because that human being killed another, and that's not justice, that's revenge. However, it's revenge only if the person charged was guilty of the crime; if later it can be proved that they were not guilty, then with the intent to kill – government legislation – the sentence, and the premeditation of taking the prisoner to the gallows, then the country (on our behalf) is guilty of murder. It's all very well to say that if there is a 1 per cent miscarriage of justice statistic then that is acceptable – unless you are one of the 1 per cent.

Inevitably, the question of the stiff penalties will present itself in the history of the Great Train Robbery, and the cry of 'Well, they did cosh the driver' will be the justification. What damage using that argument did to the driver himself can only be guessed at, but these days considering the effect of an incident on someone's heath is much more accurate and is really a prediction.

Another prediction is that we won't see the likes of the Great Train Robbery again. We'll hear about crimes involving huge amounts of money, or things of huge value, but it won't be the type of crime that will become a myth. However, the myth was actually there long before that night in August 1963, when a group of London lads out-wilded the Wild West, out-dramatised the movies, and out-mythed the myth.

ACKNOWLEDGEMENTS

There are many people to whom I am indebted for the time and trouble they have given to enable me to complete this book. I can't say some more than others because each contribution was unique.

Jonathan Reeve at Amberley Books was consistently helpful and supportive, and indeed, flexible. Claire Macdonald has been superb with her artistic creation and was a great help in reproducing the old Bucks Constabulary coat of arms. Michael Shaw, previously of Bucks Police and Thames Valley, could dig this out and many other artefacts from the past. John Bailey, police photographer, and John Woolley, police constable – both are generous to a fault. Clare George at the Post Office Museum at Mount Pleasant was also helpful. Professor Colin Divall of the University of York/National Railway Museum for addressing questions of drivers' and second man's abilities and the changeover to diesel and electric traction on BR. As well as John Bailey, Melanie Knight and David Scripps from Mirrorpix were of great help with pictures; not forgetting Garry Jackson for his D326/40326 piece. The National Association of Retired Police Officers and its branches also filled many gaps for me.

Also to Bobby and Jean Welch, Jim and Gill Hussey, Tommy Wisbey and Bruce Reynolds for the enormous help in the finer points, and Kelly Owen for her usual several hundred per cent.

INDEX